Selma's CAT

and other things that matter

A Lawyer's Intimate Conversations With His Elder Clients

A COLLECTION OF STORIES

Clifton B. Kruse, Jr.

National Academy of Elder Law Attorneys

Printed in the United States of America.
ISBN 0-615-12715-0

Published by

The National Academy of Elder Law Attorneys (NAELA)
1604 North Country Club Road, Tucson, AZ 85716-3102. (520) 881-4005

ACKNOWLEDGMENTS

"To Carolyn"

"Was that your last exam?"

My wife met me at the front door of our home and this was her greeting. It wasn't my final, Final. I was graduating from Washburn Law School, and my wife and I and our two little ones would soon be heading west, to Colorado Springs, where I had a job waiting — and a bar exam to take — the big final. But I knew what Carolyn meant.

"The last one," I affirmed, my last law school test, something, of course, she knew.

My law school colleagues and I, senior law students, demonstrating our collective sense of superiority, carried canes on the campus, identifying our status to anyone who cared. The sticks were parked in a cane rack at the top of the steps that led to Carnegie Hall, which housed the University's law school. We'd pull them out when we drifted to the coffee bar west of Carnegie by a block. And we also smoked cigars. I don't think any of us inhaled, but we flaunted our cheap and roughly made stogies, setting us apart from the younger scholars who respected this foolish tradition.

"The last one," I said again, as I entered our home, relieved that my formal education was over. "Well," my wife announced, "from now on it's either kissing or smoking."

With that announcement, I'd had my last cigar, a Hav-a-Tamp®, 2 for 15 cents as I recall — a month's supply cost 60 cents, about all the money that could be wasted by a law student with a family.

My wife's edict was proclaimed 41 years ago, and it was my last smoke, a habit endured by my mate for 6 years of graduate school, and she'd had enough of the smoke and nicotine smell.

It's my wife, Carolyn, that has made this book of stories possible. She cared for me during my last year of college, the 3 years of graduate school that followed and the 3 years of law school following that — 7 years in all. She's continued to give, enduring the long hours and my 6 day weeks at the office that a committed law practice requires. She's bright, charming, caring, and beautiful. Carolyn is, indeed, my muse, and the experiences that I've had, collected in the stories that follow, were made possible by her.

Very special appreciation is given to Sheila Allard, my legal assistant for the past decade. Her scholarly, sensitive insights and recognition of what is required of a staff in a law practice concentrated on assisting older clients, has been invaluable. She has typed, retyped and retyped again the 8 to 10 drafts of each of this book's stories required until they're just right. Without her computer skills, her love of people, her diligence in making sure I've used the right word ("dehiscement" came from her), the product would have been unworthy.

Nancy Smelser, who for almost two decades has assisted me — has typed, I believe, almost every will I've ever written, efficiently and accurately, and has taken over the work of Sheila who is retired. Nancy now types and retypes the stories which we continue to collect, documenting the fascination experienced in working with elder law clients, still 8 to 10 drafts of each — thank goodness for computers.

Appreciation, too, is given to Lois (Byler) Murauski, who for thirty years was the author's secretary, office manager and legal assistant. She's also now retired. Collectively these individuals, Sheila and Nancy and Lois, have made possible the memories we have experienced in addressing broadly the legal needs of our clients, many who are elder members of our community.

Thanks also to my law partner, Frank Lynch. He shoulders much of the work in our office enabling me to write and lecture — avocations which otherwise would not be possible, and to Harry Margolis, a Boston author and attorney who has encouraged me to initiate the process required in publishing the stories in this book. He has faithfully encouraged me to continue my writing, and I do not underestimate the importance of this stimulation.

CONTENTS

PART FIVE

PART SIX

PART SEVEN

PART EIGHT

PART NINE

PART TEN

PART ELEVEN

PART TWELVE

POSTSCRIPT

PREFACE

"Who do you think you are?
You're not the Queen of England!"

The large nursing home aide spoke harshly to her charge, a feeble widow, perhaps 70 pounds in weight, who was attempting to make her way down the crowded corridor leading to the nursing home's front door. Someone was to pick her up. She had a guest waiting, an opportunity to exit if only briefly from her inhumane habitat, and she was late. The little one, dependent upon her four-legged walker, was trying to get through the lunch crowd, her companions in this asylum created for elders, and one of its uneducated attendants singled her out for an acerbity.

"I didn't say I was," was the wee one's response, without so much as looking at her rude accuser. Her eyes were focused straight ahead on the crowd of fellow tenants in her pathway as she continued to edge her way through the bevy of wheelchairs, walkers, four-pod canes, and the feeble and enfeebled human mass lining up for noon mess.

The aide had, just before this incident, produced a stapler for me. I had exited a nearby room, where my client, dying of pancreatic cancer, had just signed his will, and I neglected to bring a fastener. She provided that, and was courteous to me; and I was now conflicted. It didn't seem timely to scold. Besides, she was the only aide around.

Her charges, similar to energetic young children, all wanted her attention, recognition of their singular problems, all crowding, creating a near gridlock in the area, a pathway that soon could not be traversed. And she was not impassive and reacted to this pressure. I winked at her and nodded but didn't smile. I don't approve but I understand, was the message. Her work is hard and her pay is minimum wage.

In the mid-1980's a diverse coterie of lawyers, perhaps two dozen, practicing in as many states, and somehow knowing that they shared a common interest — satisfying the legal needs of older people — formed a national organization. In 1988 its charter was issued and The National Academy of Elder Law Attorneys became a reality.

Unique, the practice of these lawyers concentrates on helping a population of citizens — elders who live in the communities where these agents work. Their practice is in contrast to attorneys who work in speciality areas, such as torts, real estate, tax law, and similar legal subjects. Holistic in style, all problems typically encountered by aged citizens are the topics addressed by these practitioners. Assisted living, long term care, rights to public benefits including Medicare and Medicaid, preparing simple wills, powers of attorney, and advance medical directives form the foundation of the practice of these lawyers. Zealous in their caring for a population who are viewed by many, including the elders' own family members, as near—death and not therefore seriously in need, this band of legal caregivers has become the protectors of our society's aged and needful population.

The Academy now numbers nearly 4,000 members and publishes a monthly journal informally entitled *NAELA News*. The essays in this volume first appeared in this publication in some instances under the title "President's Message" and after the author's term of office ended, continued as a column in the *News* called "Peripatetic Essayist," teaching essays — stories about elders which demonstrate an imperative morality inherent in satisfying the legal needs of older people. The essays are essentially personal, reflective prose, rather than argumentative or rhetorical. In all but one of the episodes portrayed in these essays, the stories are accurate reflections of the real-life drama that our elder population experiences. They are biographical episodes in the lives of the individuals described in the author's legal practice.

Lawyers' work with older members of our communities is interesting and moving, often emotional, particularly where pre-mortem planning is accomplished at the elder patients' bedsides. Various strategies are considered by elder law attorneys for their clients facing a diseconomy in health, including near-death gifting and empowering others to act for them when they are at this moment far removed from an earlier time when "bright-eyed and bushy-tailed" would have been descriptive of them. But such mundanity is only superficially what an elder law practice is about. Really helping a growing older population requires a much richer mixture of tasks. These include protecting elders from physical and financial abuse by their caregivers, sometimes their children, (*see* "Think of Me as the Daughter You Never Had"); overseeing the transport and placement of the once proud family patricians in long-term care centers, sometimes in group rooms in group homes, asylums from which there is no escape, (*see* "Is My Bed Still There?"); protecting aging clients from patricide, children taking their parents' property in the name of gift, removing the final vestige of dignity from the ill but not yet moribund owners, accelerating the need for public assistance, (*see* "Trusting Mikki"); educating those who have sought their lawyers' counsel against thoughtless encouragement to sign living wills which authorize "pulling the plug" if it looks to the medical community like the once-loved elder is doomed by illness or disease, (*see* "Because I Like It Here," and "My Son Wanted Me to Die!"); and watching for possible sexual abuse, physical enticement resulting in the loss of the elders' wealth, (*see* "Have You Kissed Her Yet?").

Studied elder law attorneys, credentialed by their experience, become aware of nuances in their legal work with older clients. Subtleties in speech and behavior recognized by the lawyer allow the counselor to move beyond unquestioned belief in the euphemisms their clients convey, (*see* "Take Peggy Out of My Will!"). And such lawyers become like priests and counselors in their work with the frail elder community, (*see* "Human Encounters").

These stories support what lawyers do when they work at the highest and most insightful level with those requiring protection. They listen for their clients' hidden meanings when they speak, not just what they say, (*see* "Remembering Alice," and "With No Tide and No One to Push"). Such lawyers confront questions that their clients raise about suicide, (*see* "Come Let Us Kiss and Part"). They witness behavior that is in anticipation of death, (*see* "It's All My Money" and "Three Trusts and a Will"). They observe irrational logic as elders become miserly, scrooge-like, to the detriment of values that are ultimately much more important to them, (*see* "Ellen").

This is what these stories are about — an entertaining look at lawyers who serve our country's population of elders and who protect them from persons who may be self-interested, including not just caregivers and children, but merchants as well, (*see* "You May Already Be A Winner"). It is about a class of lawyers who respect their clients' dignity, who are not cajoled by salivating family members who see the aged ones' wealth of whatever size as something to which they, the children, are somehow now entitled.

This book is about lawyers who are professionals in the classic sense, i.e., interested foremost in their clients' needs, (*see* "We Sell Cookies, Too," "Selma's Cat" and "Sugar").

Hopefully, this book conveys this message. Such lawyers are not merchants, not vendors. Their oath is to be helpful comrades, protective of the clients whom they are privileged to serve, and of those clients' values, providing for their legal needs. By the instruments that they carry (wills, advance medical directives, durable powers of attorney) and with sensitive listening ears, they make a positive difference in their clients' lives, (*see* "Human Encounters," "Hissss," and "Our Heritage, Our Mission").

As time has passed, the author's clients reading copies of the stories placed in the reception area of his law office, became interested, calling to see if any "new stories" had been copied which they might come by to pick up or which we might mail out to them. It became obvious that the humanity of many members of the professional legal community has not been understood by the public. Lawyer, to many, is synonymous with pettifogger, with the rascally ads of some who appear as mischievous merchants, and who practice law as though it were a self-interested business.

There are many lawyers who are professionally committed to making life better for the clients whom they serve. This book is dedicated to them, those lawyers who concentrate on the more humane ethic that this book illustrates.

Following a number of the stories or the conclusion of a segregated part, a postscript follows, a conclusion to the subject matter, explaining in some cases why the material is important in the practice of elder law and may serve as a transition to the materials that follow. In a few of the stories endnotes appear at the end of the chapter, somewhat in the style of Michel de Montaigne, illustrative of his technique and writing style, pithy reflections of the materials to which they relate. (*See* "Have You Kissed Her Yet?" and "Come Let Us Kiss and Part.") Other essays that are endnoted principally appeared in the stories written by the author in the "President's Column" appearing as a regular feature of *The NAELA News*, the near-monthly organ of the National Academy of the Elder Law Attorneys.

PART ONE

"Sugar"

"What will happen to 'Sugar' when I die?"

"Sugar?"

"My dog. Will you find a home for him?"

"Certainly," I perhaps too quickly replied. My client was older, becoming increasingly frail, and receiving regular doses of Medicare reimbursements. She had never married, had no children, no close relatives — a vulnerable elder. And she was preparing for her death. For her, "Sugar" was family, her child, the one accompanying her in the near-last stages of her end-life. Finding a home for the only member of her household is no different, it seemed to me, than adoption, locating successor parents for an orphaned minor.

"Sure, I can do that."

"Thank you," she sighed, "I've been really worried about this. I know that I'll die first and Sugar will be alone. If you can't find a home for him, then promise me that you'll have him euthanized — but you must be there with him when this happens."

She's expanding my promise — watch a dog die; watch him be killed. Take him to the executioner because I couldn't find a home for him? Never! And she knows this. She's clever, giving me an incentive to find her dog new digs — on this planet.

Although the ink was dry on the documents, her Last Will and other legal papers, it was only a matter of hours after our signing conference that I received a call from the police. The *gendarme* advised me that my friend had died, a self-inflicted gunshot wound was the cause. She was found in her backyard, I was told, with a note pinned to her blouse, "Call my lawyer. He'll come to get my dog." My phone number and name followed. The note was reread to me, listing the first in a series of duties I assumed in this continuing agency. Acting as her executor in this situation included faithfully fulfilling a promise.

"What kind of dog is it," I asked the uniformed caller. But he didn't know. For the first time in my rather long association with its owner, I realized that I'd never asked — what is the breed? This could be a problem. Is he vicious? Will I get jumped, pounced on when I enter *his* home? And how will I get in? I suddenly realized that I didn't have a key.

I aimed my car west on Highway 24 towards a cozy little town that borders Colorado Springs' westward edge, nearer Pikes Peak, the state's famous mountain. Manitou Springs is the entrance for those who intend to ascend it, a fourteener, framed by every window facing west in our city. Manitou sits deep into the evening shadow that the mountain's peak casts. It's a miner's town, filled with shacks and cabins on its lower slopes constructed in earlier days by the town's hard rock miners, but still used. This community was Sugar's home, where he'd comfortably lived all of his life. He and his mistress had walked its streets, past the Congregational Church a block from their home, westward from there into the village-like downtown shops, the grocery, post office, and tiny bank. Sugar accompanied his mistress whenever she allowed it, but he was never brought to my office, ten stories up in the Holly Sugar Building — too high-falutin, perhaps, with thick carpets, and long-legged leather chairs and other niceties that the four-legged ones among us might not fully appreciate.

The police gave me a key. The sergeant was trusting. I entered the home gingerly through its front door. "Here Sugar," I called out softly, not moving more than a foot inside the door, ready to make a fast getaway if a large dog appeared — or even a small one if his teeth were showing.

Into the foyer quietly walked a small, neatly groomed white toy poodle, red bow around his collar, stub of a tail furiously moving. He was greeting a friend. My client had obviously prepared him. He acted as if I were expected. It was our first meeting — instant bonding. He was freshly groomed. His mistress's death was carefully planned. A checklist was no doubt followed, near last on the long list — "Have Sugar groomed." He needed to make a good impression. He did! I picked him up and carried him to the car aimed now towards Carolyn's home, my home, a place where Sugar would be introduced to cats — large cats, Maine Coons — cats with sharp claws and with no mood for dogs — of any size.

"Here's the deal," I began as soon as the front door opened. Sugar walked on in, no need for him to tarry at the entry while I was pleading my case. He had another job to do, quietly but conspicuously marking his new found territory. He had to be sure that the big cats who live in this house are aware that Sugar is here — his home, too, at least for awhile.

"It's only for a bit," I told my wife, until *we* [I enlarged the contract] find him a home." Thank goodness she groomed him, I spoke silently to myself. He's gorgeous;

without the cats he'd have permanent quarters here.

Actually, he got along well with the Maine Coons. To begin with, they were larger and let Sugar know rather immediately what his position was in the hierarchy, at least at 4 Crossland.

But, of course, he was a bother. He liked to tease the cats and make them play chase. Cleaning supplies were regularly purchased at the supermarket, bought weekly in large quantities, and the good bedspreads, those that hang to the floor, thick and not inexpensive, were put on the high shelves for the duration. We never could get Sugar trained to go outside, to the "cob house," or to the sand box to spray. He liked to leave his scent near places where the cats hung out. This was his calling card: "You just think you're in control," was his perfumed message.

Six months passed but no one we could trust wanted a past mid-life male dog. And it was now December. Summer and Fall were history. Sugar was still part of the family, following my wife Carolyn all over the house, helping her in his own way as she washed and cleaned the areas of his markings. Sugar saw this as part of Carolyn's job, something that she, no doubt, enjoyed doing. And so he was helping.

We'd been adopted, but we were still looking for a home for him — now working on the B list. My wife is very patient, and knows also that promises are to be taken seriously, even those made in rash moments, perhaps, like the one that resulted in our caring for Sugar.

The year was ending. Christmas Eve arrived. I left the office about 4:00, stopping by Ray's Texaco to get the Subaru gassed up. Ray, a childless widower, aged himself, still pumped the gas for his customers — nothing new fangled like credit card inserts to get the pump going. There were two choices at Ray's place, mid—octane regular or unleaded. Fancy cars had to go up the street where the super unleaded ethane could be found, and where really modern pumps could disgorge several varieties of petrol, computer programmed, available by touching the right pads, complete with a printed receipt when the hose nozzle was replaced in its housing.

Ray looked down in the dumps. "Merry Christmas" didn't seem to be an appropriate greeting. He did not appear joyous. It was clear that something was wrong. "What's up, Ray?" I asked.

"My dog died. Christmas Eve, and my dog dies!" He was heart-broken. "A toy poodle . . ." He couldn't finish the sentence, and began to cry. Ray had no family. For him this was going to be a lonely, a lousy holiday. We stood close, facing each other. There's nothing to say in such a sad moment. I put my arm around him. For a few minutes we were both quiet.

"What time do you close today, Ray?"

"5:00," he said. It was now after 4:30. My home is normally 15 minutes away. "See ya' later, Ray." I drove off, speeded up when I got a block or so away, raced to get home. It was snowing, but only lightly, not an impediment. No cell phone — couldn't call home with the news, so I stopped on the way at the "7-11" and gave my wife the message. "Get out the red ribbon." That's all I had to say; she knew.

4:59. The lights at Ray's station were still on. Thank goodness that Ray is punctilious. It's not yet 5:00. He will still be there. I pulled up as Ray came out, still red-eyed, still morose.

"I forgot to get gas, Ray." He laughed; he knew. He moved towards the old Texaco pump as I opened the car door. And there he was for Ray to see — Sugar — a clone of Ray's pet. God love him, Sugar's tail was going a mile a minute, jumped over to the driver's side and gave Ray a kiss — on both hands. "Hi, friend," was his greeting. "He's yours, Ray. I've been keeping him for a friend. She asked me to give him to you," a good home where there'll be lots of love and no cats to put up with.

"Ray, he does mark — or at least he did at our place."

"You have cats!" Ray came to Sugar's defense. "Of course he marked. Come here, Sugar; come to daddy. A match made in heaven." That's how Ray explained it to me when he got the full story. "Is this what lawyers do, Clif?" Ray asked. "Indeed! This is Elder Law 101, Ray — the first thing some of us learn in law school." I drove away. A block down the street I realized — I forgot to get the tank filled — again. I looked back. The Texaco sign was no longer lighted. Sugar and his "daddy" had headed home.

"But, I'd Have to Leave Nike"

"But, I'd have to leave Nike." Nike is Bill's nine year old cat. Widowed, my client's three children are long out of the nest. Bill is now alone and his best friend is a long-haired mandarin orange colored feline, one the cat fanciers would call "a red."

Nike and his servant-master live together; their home is one among several clinging to a rocky slope on the city's western edge, part of the great Rocky Mountain foothills. Bill's and Nike's home is high enough so that the city's lights can be seen as evening comes each day. They are visible from the home's kitchen window and from the windowed pantry where Nike's food is stashed when its sliding door is open.

A modest but deep, narrow gorge is a slash at the eastern lot line's edge. This ravine carries the rainfall and the melting winter snow away from the hillside slope to an unknown destination somewhere on a lower level, perhaps to an underground, natural cistern. The water just disappears. Bill doesn't know where it goes and doesn't care. Nike knows to stay away when the runoff fills the narrow slit in the earth beside his home; so do the red foxes and an occasional gray who trample the backyard earth of the homes on Constellation Avenue where Bill and Nike live. It's a macadamed shelf that conjoins the houses of those living in the skyward loft snuggled onto the mountains' initial slope. And it's fresh, crisp mountain air that's breathed at every moment by those whose claims are staked out on the rising ground above and below the avenue's passageway.

Bill is 82 and for the past few weeks has been looking over the city's assisted living centers, the "A-L's" he calls them, those in places filled with the combined aroma of people living in a large indoor community, and those in the making, scheduled for completion soon with leasing offices on site, and colored drawings on large signs urging lookers to stop — to make deposits before the good rooms, not yet framed, are all taken.

"It'd be $3,400.00 a month just to live in one," Bill said, "with no assistance until I need it. Then the bill goes up. Holy moly, it only costs me $700.00 a month now, maybe $800.00, to live in my own home — with Nike." Bill's cat wouldn't be welcomed in an A-L, and Bill knows that.

Draft one of Bill's will had just been completed, and we met at his home to do some fine tuning. His net worth in dollar bills stacked on top of each other wouldn't reach the tallest peak in the Rocky's range within Bill's eyesight, but there would be a tall stack. How high would a pile of two million ones be?

"All my friends tell me to get me into an A-L center so I'll be ready if and when I need it." He looked at me helplessly. He needed some ammo, reasons for remaining where he is, in his home, as if leaving his beloved Nike wasn't a sufficient reason to stay put.

"Ever been on a cruise ship, Bill?" I asked, "same people every day, day after day. The cabin doors open and out they come, parading toward the breakfast buffet. Do the topics of conversation change? Do you get cornered? Do you listen to the same nonsense every day? Do you stay inside the cabin's close confines some days just to avoid the ceaseless chatter, the phatic talk, of those who have nothing to say?

"Do the people change at the A-L's? One dies or is taken to a nursing home, another arrives, one who looks and talks just about the same as the one now gone. Do I have this right, Bill? And you're a prize, a really good catch. Those looking will have their Woolworth cologne smeared on at breakfast mixed, of course, with the aroma of bath powder, a whiff of which will be enough to overcome you. It'll make the crepes less tasty. Burned toast is something you'll look for, a nosebag full, a nostrum against the freshly perfumed ones near you, those in line for seconds.

"I've never been on a cruise ship, Bill, so I'm just making this up — but can you visualize it — a room filled with the same people every day, people who have little in common except they, too, were told, as were you, that they'd better move into an A-L because they might need it someday.

"And they might, and so might you, so rent one then, not now. This is the rule, Bill: never, ever leave your home until you have no choice. Bring help to you. How much help can you have for the same price that the A-L will cost? You spend $800.00 a month now. Subtract that from $3,400.00. How much care can you get for $2,600.00 bucks a month — in your own home?

"If you need round-the-clock care, the option's yours — at home or in a nursing center; you've got the dough. Am I missing something?"

Bill leaned back in his overstuffed den chair; its lower side portions showing the effects of its double duty, used also as Nike's scratching post. His look was upward at the high ceiling which made the room imposing. He was thinking. I didn't interrupt this interlude with speech. "It's my home — and Nike's," Bill finally exclaimed. "My wife and I built it. I love it! I must be crazy. My kids are fine — two lawyers out of three kids. The bright one is into computers — the third kid." He grinned — so did I.

"Phatic talk — chatter, right? I was listening, and you're right. That's all I'd hear, and, if not perfume, an antiseptic smell . . . and institutional food."

Bill leaned back again. "Lovely!" He began an introspection, a quodlibet, his eyes shut tightly. Some of his thoughts were verbalized, but mostly the contemplation was in quiet thoughts, the good ones accentuated with a wry smile. He could, should, stay in his home with Nike, his consort; he is a king in a Rockies' castle, and he knows it.

Finally, Bill's eyes opened. "Done," he exclaimed. "I'm staying! Decision made! Why did I ever think otherwise?"

Nike took this occasion to get some stroking. He jumped up on his much loved master's lap, and he turned on his motor. Two content beings, bound to each other, reinforcing their affection. "Tell your friends that the A—L idea is history, Bill. You're at the top of the heap. Don't look down again."

#

Will drafting 412 — not a freshman class. Experience provides the stage on which elder lawyers perform, making life better for our elder clients — those who haven't listened clearly to their own hearts, who forget what life may really be like without their precious Nikes (and their replacements), consorts to their providers, and at whatever age still like infant children. They cannot be abandoned, left behind, ever forgotten.

#

Two million. That's enough for at-home care forever for Bill and his sidekick as well — if either ever needs it. It's only money given in exchange for life, for living, for joy, for the privilege of breathing mountain air, seeing the city's sky scape glowing through the night. It twinkles into Bill's and Nike's kitchen as cans are opened, their contents heated. Bill spoons up the food. Nike joins in when the scraps are attractive. For them, this is gourmet dining, feasts looked forward to and shared daily by inseparable friends.

*Selma's Cat**

Selma called. She's an independent, intelligent 89-year-old resident of the city in which I live. I could hear her crying when I picked up the phone. Between sobs, she explained that her rental home was being put on the market by its owner — and she would have to move.

"I can't move," she said. "It'll take me a year to move. I can only pack a bit each day. And I have 'stuff' everywhere."

"And my cat," she went on... a stray who comes in to eat everyday, then leaves. "He walks across the street, saunters really; he has friends there, other cats."

"Who will feed him?" she continued, acknowledging this as her personal responsibility. "I can't leave him... He nips me sometimes, real hard. I don't know why he does that."

So I called the landlord. Selma never missed a rental payment — $525 a month. She's an uncomplaining tenant in the decrepit old building, fearful, I suppose, that carping would result in increased rent. And I told him about the cat.

The landlord agreed to execute a lease — long term — even 12 years, and if he sold the house, the sale would be subject to the lease.

"Could Selma unilaterally terminate?" I asked for obvious reasons.

"Yes, she could do that."

"You're a very thoughtful man. And I'm appreciative and I know that Selma will be also."

I called Selma, feeling pretty good. Wow! This is what lawyering is about. I love this job.

"Selma," I called out over the phone — "you don't have to move." I practically yelled. "Bob, the landlord, said he'd give you a lease — long as you want — which you can break if you ever change your mind. What a deal. He really likes you. He liked the cat story, too."

"You know," she softly whispered, "he's broken the lease." What lease, I wondered; she's month to month now.

"He never fixes anything — no repairs."

"You want out?" I asked incredulously — "want to leave? Shall I call him and tell him

---

* This episode formed the author's final address to the National Academy of Elder Law Attorneys given prior to the passing of the President's gavel to his successor at the Academy's annual symposium held in Cambridge, Massachusetts, May 17, 1996. The discourse began with the following introduction: "The President's columns, the source of our communications since last July, have been primarily in essay form; not sermonic, I hope, but inspirational and moral in tone, defining what our practice is and what it can be. What does an elder lawyer do? Other lawyers ask us this question; so do our clients. Let's be guided by Selma and her August cat."

some things need nailed, some stuff fixed?"

"You know," she quietly replied, "I'm having trouble with this cat. He leaps at me with his claws out."

"You want to move?"

"It's hard for me to get around," was her dreamy reply.

"What do you want me to do now, Selma? Should I come by?"

"Don't phone before 11:00," she said. "I stay in bed until 11:00. I've hurt my back."

#

Selma, a respected journalist in her day, no longer moves from point A to point B in a straight line; perhaps she never did. But she loves her life, her hovel-like home, the independent cat that she shares with others, who bites her, no doubt, when he discovers that she has shut the outside door, temporarily confining him amid the stacks of sacred debris in the rooms and hallways of what may be, if she's lucky and doesn't have to move, her last home.

Such vignettes of life are our daily exposure as we are privileged to enter into the last homes of others:

humorous, sometimes —
sad,
enriching to us,
shaping our character,
softening our rigid assurance that we have all the answers for any who will listen.

How fortunate we are to have the age-wizened elders as clients. We learn from them — genuine people, whose lives are shared with us.

We are vignettes in their life's spectrum, too, short moments — but not forgettable by us, and perhaps not by them either.

While we do our work we learn from them. Their separate histories influence our present. And we are both enriched and better because of these encounters.

Sometimes we take our pay in 1940 dollars, or at least dollars valued higher in another age. One thoughtful but frugal lady who could no longer drive, put four cents on the dash of my car following a morning's outing, going here and there in an effort to resolve the elder's problem.

"For the gas," she thoughtfully said.

But when the bill is sent, she will pay it, less, of course, the cost of gas; that, she's prepaid.

#

Our elder clients make us better people, better lawyers. They expose us to an appreciation of a humanity we discover in ourselves that we may not have understood or felt before — and could not, except for them. During the moments that we are with them, listening — we walk in their shoes, and down the paths that their lives have taken.

Sometimes our journeys take us to the enfeebled Selmas on Bowser Street, and their cats —

loners,
fierce, independent, calling out to us, but unwilling to acknowledge that we are needed, that we have helped.

Unresponsive to our joy — they're on to other problems.

The lease is fixed;
the unwanted move is halted;
the hovel remains home;
and we don't call before 11:00.

We do our job — solving the legal problems of feeble seniors, sometimes with little credit.

Selma will continue to take care of the other pea in her pod. Selma's cat, so much like her — they are drawn to each other by their vigorously independent and proud spirits.

#

We will continue to use our skills, our imaginations, and our energy to uphold the dignity of the elders whom we serve. We will make sure that the Selmas that we know and their cats, too, are not ignored or forgotten. Their pride and independence, their self—sufficiency and dignity, are in their end-life given deserved and caring acknowledgment by us.*

* Presented as an address, the author's final comment read, "It is my great pleasure to continue with you in enviable service to the senior community. And I thank you all for the help and encouragement, the support and the warmth that you have given to me in this eighth year of our alliance."

Postscript

Pets are our client's children, seen as infants because of the care they require and the demands that they make. A 75 year old friend of mine let his cat out at 4:30 a.m. and within seconds after this early morning release, heard the makings of a cat fight. His pet was small, an adolescent, and needed protection. He turned on the outside lights and spotted "Gateway," a black and white spotted stray who had "adopted" him, high in a crab apple tree by the patio. My friend retrieved his stepladder from the basement, adjusted it under the thin, brittle tree limbs, and climbed to the highest step, shielding his eyes from being scratched by the tree's flexile spoke-like branches, and grabbed his cat saving him from a marauding tom making his early morning rounds, looking for trouble. Lawyers who work with older clients listen to their refreshing stories, the pride they have in their almost human companions. Care for their pets following the elder's death is often a crucial part of planning the elder lawyer undertakes. Pets' trusts are sometimes suggested, possible under the laws of a number of states. Some communities have organizations that find homes for pets whose owners have died. Arrangements for euthanasia are not infrequently sorrowfully made when no homes can be found.

One owner of a single cat required that her home and its furnishings be left as is for her cat whom she assumed would outlive her and would be in discomfort in any other environment. Visiting the elder in her nursing home domicile recently and referring to her home, she corrected her lawyer. "It's Fitzu's home now."

PART TWO

*"Have you Kissed Her Yet?"**

It seemed like an almost perfect solution. Elmer, a near toothless retired carpenter-mechanic, living in the city where I reside, recently lost his wife of 60 years, and his pastor, senior minister at the Assembly of God, suggested that a fortyish congregant, divorced with no children, and homeless, move in with him. She could provide care for him, prepare some of his meals, keep the house tidy, and drive him here and there in exchange for her room and board. She held a part-time job, so she had a little income. The arrangement would be without cost to Elmer, a fortuitous solution, symbiotic, a mutually advantageous association, put together by the helpful shepherd.[1]

Evelyn was provided with a separate room in Elmer's home. He respected her privacy and she, his. Not paternalistic but respectful of his age, the friendly relationship was heaven-made.

But one day, they kissed, and such a friendly gesture became more frequent. And he liked it.[2] With the passage of time, actually only a matter of a few weeks, while standing beside each other, she took his hand and placed it on her body,[3] and whispered to him that there would be much more to explore and discover, "if we marry." No *Bona Dea* she.[4]

Elmer felt flushed from the sudden adrenalin. He was flattered, aroused, and not just a bit hood-winked by the excitement of Evelyn's suggestion.[5] He had been a long-term 24-hour-a-day care provider for his wife. An invalid, she was immobile, primarily dependent on a wheelchair for movement and on Elmer, for his constant, caring and loving companionship. But now, following his wife's death, he had become the one in need. His need for compassionate care was one thing, but he was now frightened. Marriage is something that he did not need and didn't want.[6] Evelyn's tenderness,[7] with

*This chapter is endnoted. The interesting, classic references can be found at the end of this chapter.

all the energizing stimulation that now accompanied it, was understood by Elmer as self-interested, and therefore, abusive of him.

He needed help. Whom should he call? Not the good shepherd who put them together. How does one tell the priest that the interaction he has provided is an imperfect symbiont? His sons...? It would be difficult for his two big boys who loved their mama to understand their father's sudden surgence of testosterone. The family lawyer...? Perfect!

Elmer made the appointment. One son, a now-retired city policeman, came with his dad. In response to my, "What's up, guys?" opening, I was told about the caregiver, Evelyn, living in Elmer's house, arranged by the Assembly minister.

"How is it working?" I asked, knowing that it couldn't be working too well, or I wouldn't be meeting in my law office at 5:00 p.m. with two guys who just want to pass the time of day with me. "Okay," said dad.

Son shrugged his shoulders, as if to say, "Got me, I don't know." He wasn't sure why he was even here, except he provided the transport for his father.

"Is she pretty?" I hazarded a guess, which I thought might get me into the minefield where I suspected I was headed anyway, and if I were to be of help, where I needed to be.

"Yes," a mutual answer, then silence.[8]

They were both looking at me — father wondering if I had figured out yet why he was here, because he couldn't really bring himself to tell me, and son, wondering when my questions were going to go beyond cocktail party talk. There was a long silence. I guessed it was my turn again, so, I jumped in with both feet.

"Have you kissed her yet?" I said, as if such a thing were natural and expected, common between one being cared for and one providing care.

"Yes," Elmer rather matter-of-factly replied.[9]

With that, his son awoke from his late afternoon nap. He felt a surge of his own, It's a good thing Evelyn wasn't there.

"Worried about common law marriage," I inquired? (In some states, such as Colorado, its elements are cohabitation and holding one's self out to others as husband and wife. But that nicety could be explained to them later.)

"Yes," father and son spoke in unison, they were!

"What do you think should be done?" I asked and looked at father.

"Well, I don't want to marry her."

"No, you don't!" Son couldn't hold his tongue. But with the exception of what he had just heard about the kissing and such, son did like the care his dad was getting. It relieved him of an unwanted responsibility.

"Can we do a contract?" asked son, "define her duties, provide that whatever happens they won't be considered married? Can we insist that she gets nothing of Dad's, no gifts, nothing by his will? Can we transfer everything Dad owns to my brother and to me?" All reasonable, predictable — unplanned — an "I hope something can be done to save the property, to hell with Dad's feelings," kind of reaction.[10]

"What do you want, Elmer?" I asked. Elmer was scared. He's been shaking, I bet, since his hand first touched this foreign flesh. He'd had enough of this temporary fascinating predator. Let her be gone, or let her stay, but he knew, notwithstanding the temporary arousal, that he was being flim-flammed, set up, abused by one who didn't care about him, but only her own self-interests. If she stayed, there'd be no more kissing, no cheesecake, however modest, whether that had been part of the package before or not, nor anything else. "Strictly business," he said, presumably intending by this phrase, to exclude "monkey."

"Write it up," he said.

"Okay, Elmer." "But how do I do that? No touching that is fondling or like fondling, or that may lead to fondling? No cheesecake, no French maid moves?" On Elmer's part, no getting excited, stimulated, aroused — strictly business from this pretty one that he has kissed and touched before?[11] No, Evelyn needed to go. Replacement troops were needed, persons to whom predation would be foreign. There is no mast to which Odysseus can be tied; no plugs that can be run deep enough into his ears to avoid the siren's song.[12]

"Elmer," I suggested, "You call the preacher, tell him what's going on. Call Evelyn. Tell her that I want to meet with you and her, your cop-son, and with your preacher — here — tomorrow. Tell her that there is to be no more abuse of you; no more leading you on. No more super-friendly kissing. No more siren moves. No talk with endearing terms. No gifts to each other. No marriage. And, by the way, tell your son (who was sitting across the table) that there'll be no transfer of your stuff to him or to his brother, either. Elmer, are we in tune? Is this what you're telling me that you want?"

"Write it up," he said.

I don't know if he meant it. Part of him did, I suppose, but seduction is sweet and imagination without defect, and the sophistry of the temptress enduring, so that part of him, I suspect, didn't.[13]

Elmer was still shivering from the thought of what had just happened in his life, his *entre nous* into foreign intrigue. But he had allies now — his son and son's police connections, the Assembly preacher, whom I knew could be counted on to play his moral violin, and he had his own good judgment reinforced and validated. He was outsnookering a predator because Elmer was fortunately insightful and was an emotive witness to what he knew was abusive behavior by one in whom he had entrusted a confidence — and who betrayed him.

We all knew Evelyn would leave. There'd be no meeting. She'd been caught. Meet with an agent of God, the guy she tried to hustle, the guy's kid (an ex-cop), and the guy's lawyer? No way. But Elmer set it up anyway, "just in case."

I wondered in reflection the next day if this was Evelyn's *entrée* into the flim—flamming of elders' business, or if Elmer was just the next in line in her series of hopefully lucrative patsys. We probably won't ever know.

When Elmer returned to his home, the evening of his meeting with his son and lawyer, Evelyn's stuff was gone. The guest bed was made; the house was clean. A half filled cup of Souchong was on the table, a hint of lipstick on the rim.[14] It was her ignoble and soulless goodbye.[15]

ENDNOTES TO "HAVE YOU KISSED HER YET?"

1. "Whom the nuptial torch with welcome light has joined," — Catullus (Caius Valerius Catullus, 84 B.C., Roman poet), "On some verses of Virgil," Michel de Montaigne, quoted in Phillip Lopate, *The Art of the Personal Essay*, Anchor Books, (1994), p. 69.
2. "I know the traces of the ancient flame." — Virgil, also Vergil; Publius Vegilius Maro, 70 B.C., reported to be greatest of the Roman poets.) *Id.*, p. 66.
3. "And pressed her naked body unto mine." — Ovid, *Id.*, p. 96.
4. Originally a Roman goddess of chastity, *Id.*, p. 76.
5. "The goddess ceased to speak, and snowy arms outflung
   Around him faltering, soft fondling as she clung.
   He quickly caught the wonted flame; the heat well—known
   Entered his marrow, ran through every trembling bone.
   Often a brilliant lightning flash, not otherwise,
   Split by a thunderclap, runs through the cloudy skies.
   He spoke, Gave the embraces that she craved; then on her breast, Outpoured at last, gave himself up to sleep and rest. – Virgil, *Id.*, p. 67.
6. "Sweeter it is to me to live with neck unyoked." — Maximianus (Marcus Aurelius Valaerius Maximianus, Roman emperor, died 310 by suicide), *Id.*, p. 69.
7. "'Tis you she holds, but sighs for other, absent loves." — Tibullus, *Id.*, p. 99.
8. Psychologists refer to this phenomena of indirection as "coded disclosure." Hints are given on which the interviewer (lawyer) must pick up. *See* Holly Ramsey—Klawsnik, Ph.D. "Interviewing Elders for Suspected Sexual Abuse: Guidelines and Techniques, 5 *Journal of Elder Abuse and Neglect*, No. 1, (1993), p. 5.
9. " . . . she gave . . . furtive favors in the black of night." — Catullus, *supra* n. 1.
10. "Put on a lock, confine her. But then who will guard the guards themselves? 'Your wife is shrewd; with them she'll start.'" Juvenal, (Decimus Januius Juvenalis, 1st — 2d cent. A.D., Roman satiric poet), *Id.*, p. 85.
11. "Would God that as I dream of you I might behold you, And press sweet kisses on your altered locks, Take your worn body in my arms and thus enfold you!" — Ovid, (Publius Ovidius Naso, 43 B.C., Latin poet.), *Id.*, p. 110.
12. Homer, *Odyssey* Book XII, Scylla and Charybdis, Penguin (1946), pp. 189, 193.
13. "There is still some remnant of heat and emotion after the fever." Johannes Secundus, *supra* n. 1.
14. "As the Aegean, when those winds have died
    Which only lately made it churn and leap,
    Does not at once grow calm, or put aside
    The roar and violence of the raging deep."

— Tasso, (Torquato Tasso, 1544-95, major Italian poet and tragic figure of the Renaissance.), *Id.*, p. 66.

15. There is minimal literature on sexual abuse of elders. An 89-year old emaciated 70 pound resident of a nursing center, housed in a private room there, told me that she had trouble sleeping notwithstanding her regimen of nightly sleeping medication, because someone would come in at night, remove the bedcovers, and look at her. This disquieting event, real or imagined, disclosed to the administrator, resulted in replacement staff being assigned to her wing in the institution. This change resulted in no further reporting by the elder of the theretofore frequent voyeurism, suggesting that the periodic event was not imagined. For additional studies on sexual abuse of older persons, *see* Malcom G. Holt, "Elder Sexual Abuse in Britain: Preliminary Findings," 5 *Journal of Elder Abuse and Neglect*, No. 2, (1993), p. 63, 64. Holt defines sexual abuse as coercion to sexual activity." Such a definition is too narrow because it excludes voyeuristic activity. In Holt's study, 90 percent of the victims of sexual abuse, as he defines that term, were dependent upon their abusers for care. *See also* Holley Ramsey-Klawsnik, *supra* n.1, p. 5. She describes assault, (battery) during bathing of patients. She defines sexual abuse as activities wherein "an individual is forced, tricked, threatened, or otherwise coerced into sexual contact of any type against his or her will." It is wrongful physical contact, offensive touching. *See Mason v. Cohn*, 438 NYS 2d 462, 464 (S.Ct. N.Y. County, 1981), cited in *Blacks Law Dict.* Sixth Ed. (1990), p. 152. *The Journal of Elder Abuse and Neglect* can be obtained from Haworth Press, 10 Alice Street, Binghamton, NY 13904-9981.

*You May Already Be a Winner**

"I've won a million dollars," Laura G announced in a rather matter-of-fact tone. She was calling me by phone, summoning me to her home — in a voice that sounded as authoritative as a subpoena.

It was 10:00 a.m. "Are you opening your mail, Laura G?" I asked. I knew she was. I'd received the same calls from her before — many times — informing me that such a prize had been won. But I respond to subpoenas and I knew that I'd just gotten one. "I'm on my way," I reported, and I headed to the 10th floor stairwell, 11 floors down to the parking garage where my old but trusty Subaru was stored.

Some of us, I suspect most of us, become increasingly vulnerable as we age — open to suggestion by people we don't know, but who appear to be trustworthy. The faces of well-known entertainment personalities grace[1] both television and printed advertisements. The shills are charming, believable personalities. Their appearances suggest that they are insightful persons whom we can trust, and that the products they endorse will be beneficial. Bright yellow envelopes containing magazine subscription forms, for example, advise their recipients — often on the covers of the mailings on which the believable personality's image appears, that "You May Already Be a Winner." The decoy entices the readers (or the watchers of the tv ads, where that media is used,) into purchasing what the Philistae[2] are selling, often a condition precedent to claiming the prize.

When I arrived at Laura's modest but well-appointed and cleanly kept home, in neat piles on her den desk — an old card table that still served her well — now nearing a half-century of use, were 33 "You're A Million Dollar Winner," envelopes, all stuffed and waiting to be opened, a pile of stamps and envelopes were at the ready when today's paperwork was completed.

"Just came in the mail today!" she announced with enough emphasis that anyone listening would know these missives were being treated with deference. They were important. Each one was addressed to her, Ms. Laura G. She'd received them before, but she'd forgotten.

I hesitated to touch the fresh mail. Laura seemed a bit suspicious that I might take one of what seemed to her to be much like Cashier's Checks, mail them back properly filled out and one receives the money by return mail, or at least, Laura believed, that is what should happen. By the time the responses were returned to their senders, however, or at least, with the passage of a few days from the time she dutifully complied with the sponsor's instructions, Laura had forgotten that she'd even received the invitations

* This chapter is endnoted. Comments by the great 16th century French essayist, Montaigne, remain relevant in the current millennium and can be found at the end of this chapter.

to share in this wealth. I, too, was hesitant to touch a single envelope, even when, one by one, they were handed to me, afraid that Laura would suggest that I keep one, like an assignment to me, a contingency fee, play money rather than real, although Laura didn't know that. And money didn't matter to her. She was a millionaire, after all. She had today's stuffed envelopes, more than enough for her, to prove it.[3]

Today's mailings were all sent from the same magazine sales company, all were brightly colored, all with the same television talk show second banana's face on the envelope, all with magazine subscription forms to be filled out inside. While magazine purchases are optional, the form must be returned to its sender, the requirement to get into the pool of winners from which, I suspect, at some point in time, a single name is drawn. The more forms sent in by their recipients results in a greater chance of winning, or so one might suppose.

"She works at this every day,"[4] her caregiver told me, as she, although uninvited, walked into the room, an agency lady who witnessed this in other homes with other elders before. "She is sometimes still up at 1:00 a.m. working on these entries, and gets angry with me if I check on her." She spoke in a scolding way about Laura and was looking to me for some support. "It's good for her," I said, "She sleeps too much anyway." The care provider retreated. I reseated myself by Laura's desk.

"Ed McMahan was here," Laura told me in a matter-of-fact sort of way, as she began to slowly open the first of the 33 envelopes, savoring the experience.

"In your home?"

"Yes."

"When?" I asked.

"The other day — the neighbors told me. He rearranged the magazines on my coffee table."

I glanced at the weighty and neatly stacked piles of *Popular Mechanics*, *Field and Stream*, and other titles of the unread, mint—condition publications. "They were messed up?" I inquired.

"He rearranged them," she replied.

"How'd he get in?" I countered, but she didn't know. Persons like Ed McMahan, I suppose, just have their ways.

I paused a moment, not knowing whether I should keep this conversation going on not; it certainly wasn't leading anywhere, but I did. I chanced one more parry. "Why did he come here?" I asked.

"Because I've won a million dollars."

I'd had enough. She was convinced that her delusions were real.[5] Except for what I assumed was a considerable outlay of money for unread publications, they weren't causing her harm, and were a source of joy, in her case probably worth the price.

Later, however, I wrote a letter to Ed McMahan and told him what was occurring in the life of one elder living in one city in this country. While this client could, perhaps, afford the subscription purchases she was making, I hypothesized, most could not, and very likely assumed that, notwithstanding the "You don't have to order to become a winner," notice, that subscribing certainly must improve one's chances. Playing the role of decoy, which he did, I suggested while perhaps lawful, should be reexamined by persons of stature, such as he. I received no reply.

Laura continued her homework.[6] She called me; it's her move. I just sat by the table and watched her. I thought that she might have forgotten that I was there — but she hadn't. The silence created no anxiety in either of us. Finally, she spoke, not looking up from her work.

"My stockbroker is going to get my house."

"What?" I said with some surprise.

"He loves it," she told me. "He brought his wife and little girl here to see me," she continued.

The house was a small two-bedroom home, clean and kept in good condition, but in an older part of the city with small lots restraining home value. The house would sell for $60,000.00 or $70,000.00, I supposed. Certainly her broker, his wife, and their child would find it inappropriate for them, too confining. He's after a devise that he can sell, I quietly assumed, something that he could put into the market for himself.

My friend was mentally diminishing, her savvy near zero. She had been an exceptional legal secretary during a long career with one of the city's prominent lawyers — the one everyone who had much wealth went to see. She did most of the lawyering for him as far as I could tell, at least she did when I called on her boss. He was seldom seen. "Laura will take care of it," he always said, as though what I was bringing over to work out was small potatoes — unworthy of his time. I got along with Laura well — and if she was the agent with whom I was to deal, where the case involved his office, that was okay with me. He, of course, always eventually signed off on whatever we did, but I don't know if he ever read it. He trusted Laura's judgment. I was just a neophyte; she could handle me.

Never married and now retired with her lifetime employer long deceased, she called me one afternoon. "I need a will," she said, can you come by?" She never saw my office, I always went to her place, or after her retirement, on her personal business, to her home. At each visit we always sat at the same card table I was sitting by now. We have mutual respect for each other, and it is hard for me to see Laura in her decline.

"He loves it," she said again. That pleased her, her broker "loving" her home.

"Remember the line, "Oh, I just love your home." The right emphasis needs to be put on the "Oh" part — a pause after it's said, and it needs repeating on each visit so that she remembers to tell her lawyer when a new will is made, that the home is to go to the broker. I knew it wasn't right — a broker ingratiating himself with his customer — one with no family — no one likely to discover the deception; no one who regularly watches over her business affairs.

"Let me see your portfolio," I said to Laura. "Last year's tax return will have on it what I need to see." She didn't question the request, didn't ask why. The large envelope was produced — 36 stock trades in the prior year — three a month. I called the broker.

"How's Laura's account?" I asked.

"Okay," he said. "Fine, well invested."

"How many trades this year?" I asked.

Silence. He didn't want to talk anymore.

"Laura tells me that you want her house," I said.

He got the message. I showed Laura what her trusted broker was doing. She knew about churning — but it had to be pointed out. She removed the account from that brokerage that day.

On my next visit to Laura G's home I asked her if she remembered doing guardianships with me — back in the good old days. She even corrected me: "Guardianships *and* conservatorships," she emphasized. "Do you think," I questioned, "that when you get older it would be helpful if you had that set up for you, already in place in case you need it?"[7]

And she did. She could be the petitioner asking the court to appoint someone she trusted to help with decisions. The bank, for example, could take care of paying her bills and help her invest her money. Silver Key, the agency in Colorado Springs that helps elders with just about any problem they might encounter, and Mikki Kraushaar, its Executive Director who received the National Academy of Elder Law Attorneys' prestigious President's Award, could be her guardian.

Laura was familiar with the probate court, with the judge's supervision of those who handled decisions for others in need. She was familiar with powers of attorney, but who could her agent be? She didn't know anyone well enough — "but you," she said. And she realized that I wouldn't be around forever either — and we couldn't come up with anyone she trusted enough to be an alternate — although, she thought, "my broker could." The thievery was forgotten already. Her present memory was just not what it needed to be. No, clearly, Laura needed more high-powered authority than an agency — one evidenced by a court order — an agent wouldn't do.

The Latin *vulnerare* means to wound, and is the source of our word vulnerable. Seniors are a vulnerable community, and those who are frail make them singular candidates for avaricious predators to harm. They are singled out — sent "You're a Winner" letters that makes them losers once they respond. These elders put trust in others, often those they barely know — or don't know at all, but the appearance of such persons, when seen, and their voices when heard, are friendly and invite trust. Television has made that possible and the aging of our population is like a well-stocked pond, making fishing by the rapacious among us, easy.

Laura's possessions may have been salvaged — so that her remaining wealth will pass to her charities, accomplished in part without destroying her daily joy that is experienced in her den on her aging card table. You see, she "may already be a winner," and she knows that. She's convinced of it, so her conservator transfers a small amount of money into her personal account each month. And in this way, her pleasure can continue — enough so that the daily mail and its brightly-colored yellow envelopes can continue. We made sure of that — have that in a court order.

And she is protected now, also from the "Oh, I just love your home," (so leave it to me) thieves, who preen themselves in the hallway mirrors as they arrive in their patsies' homes, prideful that their offense is nearing fruition, that their predacious deception will be undiscovered.

I returned to my office knowing that across the country that day other lawyers helping their older clients were experiencing a similar sense of satisfaction — not euphoria, but comfort in the knowledge that we made a positive difference in someone's life that day.

Several days before I last met with Laura G, I watched *60 Minutes*. A case was featured where sulfuric acid spilled into the atmosphere of a California town. Lawyers and their agents descended upon the populace, signing them up for financial recovery for their collective injuries — anxiety caused by the anticipation of potential illness from the atmosphere contaminated by the tortfeasor. One hundred fifty million dollars was paid by the company involved — fifty million to the lawyers. The average recovery by the uninjured individuals, some of whom had not even been in the environs when the accident happened, was $1,700.00. A lawyer involved in the proceedings vehemently defended the law agents' work — creating a problem where none existed, filling the hospital emergency room spaces following the incident because a doctor's letter that they had been seen following the accident, physical injury or not, was a threshold required by the runners recruiting the "injured" for the anticipated class action. I don't mean to suggest that the *60 Minutes* version of the incident is incorrect — nor that I know more than what appeared on Channel 5 in my city, which carries NBC, but on my return to my office following my visit with Laura G, I was glad that I'm here, in this quiet town, filled with people with real problems, where lawyers, my colleagues and I, concentrate principally on our clients' needs, not on our personal financial interests.

I hadn't talked to Laura about a fee for the work I was to do for her — setting up the contingency guardianship, and for the morning house call, but it's second in line, to be considered after her problem is resolved. *60 Minutes* won't hear about this case, or its companions — elders across the country sitting at their card tables imagining themselves wealthy because important, "You May Already Be a Winner," letters came to them causing real injuries, loss of resources necessary to their well being. Such hoodoo occurs perhaps because of something the *60 Minutes* station themselves may do by selling advertising time to shills who sell the contents that come in yellow envelopes — promises made with fingers crossed, with a king's X, with false promises — an acid spill affecting susceptible elders in all 50 of our states, for which we can safely predict NBC will take no responsibility.

ENDNOTES

1. "The graces" in Greek mythology were beautiful goddesses, daughters of Zeus, personifying, among other qualities, intellectual and moral attributes. The persona described by the term grace is pleasing, an attractive feature, and seductive. See "Grace," The Oxford Encyclopedic English Dictionary (3d ed. Oxford Press 1996), p. 606.
2. Philistae (sometimes spelled Philetai) were early assassins. See Seneca, cited in Montaigne, "On solitude," The Essays: A Selection, Penguin, Trans. & Edited by M.A. Screech, p. 105. Montaigne wrote, "Most pleasures . . . tickle and embrace us only to throttle us, like those thieves whom the Egyptians called Philistae."
3. " . . . [n]othing is so firmly believed as whatever we know least about." Montaigne, "Judgements on God's ordinances must be embarked upon with prudence," Id., p. 93.
4. " . . . very old but still with some sap in [her]." Montaigne, "On the affection of fathers for their children," Id., p. 156.
5. "I do not believe that a soul with seared scars could have counterfeited such assurance." Montaigne. "On conscience," Id., p. 146.
6. " . . . [Because] age has lately robbed me of those [things] more pleasing to my fancy. I am training and sharpening my appetite for those which are left, more suitable to my later season." Montaigne, "On solitude," Id., p. 106.
7. "Preparing . . . for our own withdrawal [from other than passive participation in the human community] is no light matter." Id., p. 101.

*"Think of Me as the Daughter You Never Had"**

"I told her to think of me as the daughter she never had," the caregiver, who referred to herself as "the nurse," commented. She was calling to tell me that her charge had passed away that morning.

The decedent had no family in this country. She lived alone in hermit-like isolation and only in the last several weeks prior to her death did she condescend to her physician's direction, that she get help in her home if she were to remain there — or else.

Our name was left at a local funeral home by our client with instructions to call us when she died. "The 'nurse' is coming in at 11:00 to make the arrangements," I was advised by the mortuary director. "I suppose that's okay; she has no family. Her 'nurse' is closer to her than anyone, like family, she told us."

While the funeral cost was prepaid, the "family" limo was not. That, and other niceties ordered by the caregiver added $675.00 to the bill. I wondered, upon discovering this, what the eventual claim for making these arrangements would be from the "I'm like a daughter to her" caregiver.

"Did she change her will?" I was asked by the caller-caregiver on the day of the funeral. I imagined that the call was coming from the cellular phone located in the passenger section of the limo as it made its way down Highway 85 following the hearse toward its destination with its contents — a sole, hapless, "almost daughter" of the decedent. And in symmetric metaphor, also riding alone in the mortuary's hearse, rested the body of the childless elder.

Ripe for plucking, but not yet plucked — a too-soon death for the plot to reach maturity — no new will revised to include the "think of me as the daughter you never had" child. The elder's heirs in this instance are lucky.

Others have been less fortunate. A widow who, by deprivation, had saved and managed an estate approximating two million dollars, left most of her net worth to a neighbor's caregiver who checked in on the miserly 93-year old daily, "just to be sure that you're all right, Honey." Ingratiating herself to the elder, ultimately moving into the elder's home, she created a closed dependency.[1] "You only need me," was the message. She ridded herself of the elder's lawyer because that lawyer refused to provide in the elder's will for a revision of her long-standing objects of bounty, replacing devisee-charities with her new-found friend, the "voluntary" caregiver.

---

* This chapter appeared in the NAELA News, published by the National Academy of Elder Law Attorneys, and is addressed to lawyers practicing elder law. For this reason, as you have seen, some references such as "As lawyers who work with frail elders ..." and "we can see ..." are appropriate in that context. This story is endnoted. The notes can be found at the end of this chapter.

"He'll put you in a nursing home," the elder was told about her lawyer, and the elder's will was soon revised by counsel friendlier to the suggestion that the estate be left largely to the new and helpful friend. The predator-in-waiting shut the doors to all outsiders. Accounts were changed into joint tenancy with the caregiver "for convenience" and the coup was successful when the elder then in her mid-nineties died — a million a year for two years' work. And no one complained. And no one knew. Intended beneficiaries named in voided testamentary documents including revocable trusts are often unaware, and absent statutes (if such exist), receive no notice of trust or court proceedings.[2]

In April 1990 the Subcommittee on Health and Long-term Care of the U.S. House of Representatives published its findings.[3] The document entitled, *Elder Abuse: A Decade of Shame and Inaction*, reports that, in the course of its investigation "...the Subcommittee... discovered literally hundreds of examples which fall into the category of financial exploitation."[4]

Misappropriation is accomplished by force, stealth, deceit, misrepresentation and fraud.[5] The theft is sometimes swift and at other times occurs over years following the redraft of the elder's testamentary documents, with patience accompanying the stealthful plunder.[6]

Financial predators initiate their abuse by winning the elder's trust. They bring in groceries, care for the lawn, run errands and perform other tasks that the senior is unable to accomplish without help. With no relatives, or none nearby, shutting out friends, the self—interested caregiver becomes the elder's primary, if not only, source of affection. Bonding and dependency occurs. Intimacy increases between the aging elder and his or her predator. Frailty keeps the senior at home and activities necessary in daily living are provided by the thief-in-waiting — exiting from bed, dressing, eating, toileting, bathing, and managing other daily needs.[7]

Demands by the invader may follow. Terrified of being abandoned and forced into life in a dreaded nursing home, relying on hopeless promises mouthed as needed by the abuser, property is conveyed; joint accounts are opened; revocable trusts are created and funded, sheltered as they are from easily accessible court review, avoiding even the notice to heirs requirement that a probated will assures.

In representing elderly clients who are frail and susceptible to caregiver influence,[8] should we intervene when we observe or suspect financial (or other) abuse of our client? Should we alert family or an appropriate court so that the county's adult protective services, or a court—appointed temporary fiduciary, such as a guardian-ad-litem, can investigate and initiate protective intervention? The *American College of Trust and Estate Council (ACTEC) Commentaries*, affirming the intent of *The Model Rules of Professional Conduct*, (for lawyers) 1.14, suggests that we may. Our own consciences suggest a stronger verb be used in this statement: We should! *The Commentary* reads:

> If the lawyer believes that the best interests of the disabled person requires representation by an independent party, the lawyer may suggest to a family member or to an appropriate tribunal that a guardian-ad-litem or another lawyer be appointed for the disabled person[9] [so that such person's interests will not be compromised].

This intervention may occur, presumably, notwithstanding the affected person's reluctance.[10]

Model Rule 1.14(b)[11] addressing "client[s] under . . . disability, and the source of *The ACTEC Comment*, provides that a lawyer may seek the appointment of a guardian or take other protective action with respect to a client . . . when the lawyer reasonably believes that the client cannot adequately act in [his or her] own interest.

This rule allows a lawyer to exercise discretion in initiating protective action to abate actual or anticipated harm to a client. In such intervention the lawyer acts as a de facto guardian for the client.[12] In this *milieu* the attorney may consult physicians concerning a client's suspected disability so that both the lawyer and physician may be better informed with the intention of helping an individual over whom they share common responsibility.[13] And further, the lawyer may contact family members or "...an appropriate tribunal [to request] that a guardian-ad-litem or another lawyer be appointed [to protect] the disabled person,"[14] at least in those states that acknowledge the legitimacy of this Rule.[15] The compatriot Model Rule imposing an obligation to honor client confidences is obeisant, secondary to the victimized party's protection.[16]

As lawyers who work with frail elders, we are aware that older people anticipating the need for skilled level care will do literally anything to avoid transfer from their homes to the "coffin—ships," the institutional homes envisioned as ships of death.[17] This reality makes our clients vulnerable, ripe for plucking, by a community of self-interested home-care providers — by whatever name.[18]

Whether it is a young lover who has made another starry-eyed, or an elder where affection from her caregiver results in similar dependent bonding — both look up to the one providing affection. Both who appear cared for may only be satisfying the self-interest of the one providing what is, to the young, perceived to be love, and to the elder, believed to be sincere affection. But, both young and old are similarly charmed in order to satisfy the self-interested predation of their abusers.

"Tales from the Front,[19]" a syndicated column appearing weekly in a number of this country's newspapers, focuses on the transitory life of young love. Primarily written for thirty-something teenagers who tattle on themselves and witness their unquiet desperation to presumably eager, voyeuristic readers, the message is clear. The ones they have loved are gone and the writers feel abandoned, double-crossed, deceived, exposed, used and hurt, worse off than they were before the tragic relationship began.

The elderly, too, are similarly preyed upon by some in the community of unlicenced care givers where self-interest is not secondary to the purpose of their employment. The home-bound elders imagine that what superficially appears as real affection for them provided by their avaricious companions is genuine. The frail elderly are often lonely, and long to be cared for, to be loved, even to be touched. They overlook the signs of their provider's self-interest; they do not sense the stealth in their new-found companions and are stimulated to reward their end-life care provider with generous largesse.

"Think of me as the daughter you never had," epitomizes the simplicity that allows the insidious theft. "No ship of death for me. My 'daughter' will provide." The unspoken nunc pro tunc in this surreptitious relationship is the appropriation by gift or devise of the elders' worldly goods by their crafty, uncaring, and treacherous companions.

The lawyer's Model Rule for appropriate conduct, 1.14, in its most altruistic sense, imposes upon us a responsibility, a devotion to others' interests, and at minimum provides an ethical protection, a bulwark from the obligation we otherwise have as lawyers not to breach our clients' confidences. We can, therefore, comfortably see this Model Rule as an opportunity to better protect the interest of our charges, the consummate responsibility in every event of all lawyers.[20]

ENDNOTES TO "THINK OF ME AS THE DAUGHTER YOU NEVER HAD"

1. By dependency is meant that none other could enter into this relationship; none other can help. It is a relationship that excludes all others who would otherwise interfere in the symbiotic relationship. *See*, "Golden Age Prey," *Gazette Telegraph*, Colo. Spgs., Colo. 7-11-93, p. G-1, 4; "Isolated and Lonely, the Home-Bound Elder is 'Ripe for Exploitation'." *See* Liza and Burby, "Financial Abuse of the Elderly Spreads," *New York Times*, Jan. 2, 1994, at 13 LI-1, cited in Bill Labovitz, "Memorandum — An Act to Prevent Financial Exploitation of Elders," Boston Univ. School of Law, Legislative Services Clinic, 5-13-94, p. 21, n. 106.
2. This is an argument, perhaps, for probate attorneys and trustees of revocable trusts to be required to put beneficiaries named in prior testamentary and trust documents on notice of abatements of devises made in prior estate plans caused by near—death testamentary revisions. In this way, issues involving undue influence made possible by confidential relationships arising during the elder's period of frailty could be examined and the harm caused by predators lessened.
3. *Elder Abuse: A Decade of Shame and Inaction*, Subcommittee on Health and Long-Term Care of the Select Committee on Aging, House of Representatives, 101st Congress, Second Session, April 1990. The report is found in Comm. Pub. No. 101-752, U.S. Gov't. Printing Office, Washington, D.C., (1990). *See also* "Civil Remedies to Enhance Protection of Vulnerable Adults from Financial Exploitation," Rpt. of the Virginia Bar Assn., House Docu. 24, Commonwealth of Va. (1990). (Available through ACTEC Elderlaw Committee, March 1996, Meeting Report, 3415 So. Sepulveda Blvd., #460, L.A., CA 90034.)
4. Subcommittee Rpt., *Id.*, p. 11.
5. *Id.*
6. Additional examples of financial exploitation are set out, *Id.*, pp. 15-16.
7. Debbie Warhola, "Victimized! Seniors are Easy Prey;" *Gazette Telegraph*, Colorado Springs, Colorado, May 26, 1994, Section E-1, Rick Ansorge, "Golden-Age Prey," *Gazette Telegraph*, Colorado Springs, Colorado, July 11, 1993, Section G-1, 4; Judy Keen and Maria Goodavage, "Depleting the Life's Savings is a Big Fear," *USA Today*, May 13, 1993, p. 1.
8. *See* C.B. Kruse: "Elder Care and Contracts to Devise," *Probate Practice Reporter*, Vol. 7, No. 4, (April 1995), p. 1; "Contracts to Devise or Gift Property in Exchange for Lifetime Home Care — Latent and Insidious Abuse of Older Persons," *Probate Law Journal*, Vol. 12, No.1, (1994), p. 1. "Contracts to Devise or Gift Property in Exchange for Lifetime Home Care — Blatant and Insidious Abuse of Older Persons," Lecture, National Academy of Elder Law Attorneys, Chicago, Il., (November 1992).

9. *ACTEC Commentaries*, *supra*, p. 134.
10. *See* Michael Gilfix, "Representing the Elderly Client," *Trial*, (November 1994) pp. 80-81.
11. *See ACTEC Commentaries on the Model Rules of Professional Conduct*, (2d Ed. on March '95), M.R.P.C. 1.14, p. 131 ff.
12. *The ACTEC Commentaries* observe that the rule, as originally proposed, required the lawyer to take protective action. Id., p. 132. See ABA Probate and Trust Subcouncil, Response to *Kutak Commission*, 9 *Prob. & Prop.* 6, 9 (1981).
13. *See* ABA Informal Opinion 89-1530, appearing in *The ACTEC Commentaries*, *supra* n.11, p. 133.
14. *ACTEC Commentaries*, *id.*, p. 134. The *Rule's* last phrase reads, " . . . for the disabled person," which the author interprets to mean "to protect."
15. *See Mich. RI 76*; Neb. Op. 91-4 (1991); Or. Op. 1991-41; Pa. Op. 91-36 (1991); 90-89 (1990); Ala. Op. 87-137 (1987); 90-12 (1990); NYC Op. 1987-7 (1987). *Contra*; Cal. F. Op. 1989-112 (1989); Cal. (LA) Op. 450 (1988); Annots. Collected in *ACTEC Commentaries*, *id.*, pp. 134 ff.
16. *M.R.P.C.* 1.6. Imposing an obligation to honor client confidences is obeisant, secondary to the victimized party's protection.
17. Nursing homes are imagined to be ships of death, unseaworthy ships by those who anticipate steerage. *See* "Coffin Ships," *Webster's Third New International Dictionary*, (Miriam Co. 1966), px. 440.
18. *Supra*, n.1.
19. Chery Lavin, syndicated columnist, *Chicago Tribune*.
20. One who acts to protect and enforce the legal rights of another is engaged in the practice of law. This is what lawyers do. *See Denver Bar Ass'n. v. Public Util. Comm'n.*, 391 P2d 467 (Colo.1964).

"God Does Work Wondrous Things"

Her deceased husband had been a man of rank, an officer retired from the United States Air Force, and this made it possible for her to be admitted to the Air Force Academy Hospital in Colorado Springs. Her friend called me using the phone on the bedside table in my client's private room in this small facility. It's located a short distance from the cadets' football field, planned, perhaps, for quick ambulance runs necessary sometimes when the smaller cadets play teams such as Notre Dame. "Mrs. Peterman needs to see you. Can you come?"

When I arrived I learned that my client had undergone an abdominal cancer operation; she wasn't doing well. The surgical wound oozed fluids. Mucous would accumulate in her mouth requiring an attendant, or her visitor, if such person were willing, to take gauze and clean the cavity every few minutes. The frequency increased when visitors were present because she tried to communicate even though she was unable to speak. Her lips and mouth would move but no voice could be heard. She communicated with a small chalkboard, and when it was not possible for her to write her thoughts, or the word was not decipherable, an alphabet board could be used to spell out her message. A bedside guest such as I learned patience from visits such as this, and in communicating, an economy of words are used.

Gladys Peterman, Mrs. P. to me, had been a client of mine for many years. I was with her when Harold, her retired officer-husband died. I knew the nature of her assets, her nearest relatives, her values. I brought her file with me to this meeting, reviewed matters with her and received most answers with just nods. But after going through this history with her comfortably and surprisingly quickly, I asked her if she could give me a clue about today's topic — using a word or two, spelling something out on her board; and she could.

"CD," she wrote, "stolen." then a person's last name, someone unknown to me.

"Bank?" I responded, starting to shorten sentences into words myself. "What bank issued the CD?"

She wrote out its initials, "CNB."

"Okay, I'll go to the bank, get a print-out of what you currently have deposited there and see if it differs from what the bank held in your name a month or so ago, and see if I can determine from this what was taken. Do you have a favorite teller? Yes?" She nodded. "Okay — can you write out that name?"

"Anna." Her writing was clear, although it took a painfully long time for her to write even a single alphabetic letter.

I called the bank and not a short time later Anna was traced and was on the phone.

I explained the situation. Anna knew that Mrs. P. was in the hospital; that helped. From the hospital I headed to the bank. The teller had the print-outs — and more. She had a copy of a replacement CD, one reissued to replace the one that matured, stolen by Mrs. P's friend, a bachelor near her in age who had been courting Mrs. P. before she became ill. When Mrs. P's CD had come due, a replacement CD was issued in her friend's name.

"How could this have happened?" I asked. Anna didn't know, but the paperwork was otherwise perfect, tracing the CD purchased from the proceeds of Mrs. P's certificate which had matured and was reinvested — but in her friend's name alone. I never did discover why the bank allowed this. We protected this from happening again, however. I took over for my client as a de facto agent, paperwork to follow. Small town, Colorado Springs, even smaller when this happened, and the bank knew where to find me if I steered them wrong. My office was across the street, Suite 300 at the First National. The bank was also probably grateful that I wasn't yelling at them for what appeared to be a slip-up — a potential costly goof by someone who worked in the bank, an employee whose name the bank didn't share. I didn't ask either, no reason for me to know. The problem was solved. The CD was subject to a hold order until I got the paperwork necessary to void the surreptitious theft.

I called the thief, someone I'd never met. "Jack," I said, as if we were old friends, "meet me at the CNB in thirty minutes; bring the 'CD.'

"What CD?" he replied. I gave him the number. I had the bank's copy in front of me. "And bring your pen," I said sternly. "I'm using that term in the sense of a writing instrument. Comprehend?" He understood.

"N. H.," Mrs. Peterman wrote on the chalkboard — her shorthand for nursing home. We had no trouble deciphering those letters. This was expected. The social worker staff at the Academy were making the arrangements and reviewed them with me when I called. Colorado Springs had no Hospice center when these events were happening or she would have been headed there. She was terminal, requiring constant attendants, morphine, mouth swabbing, comfort care, medical help that was palliative. There was no cure for the insidious illness and the damage it caused in her body.

I had just told Mrs. P. that the CD was in her name again, when suddenly in walked Jack. He was slimy, predacious, a coxcomb, unrepentant.

"Tell Mrs. P. what you did, Jack," I said.

"She wanted me to have it, didn't you, Sweetie?" He leaned over, kissing her cheek; a smoodge, he stroked her hair. Mrs. P. didn't look pleased. She was rigid in her bed but had no room to move; she was trapped, had no way to leave and no ability to verbally object.

"I'm going to court, Jack. Mrs. P. will have a guardian-conservator by tomorrow."

I was going in to get emergency orders, immediate protection, perhaps a restraining order against this parasitic nematode. I dictated the pleadings on the way from the hospital after I left Mrs. P.

I underestimated Jack. It was Friday — no way to get the protective order until Monday; that gave him two days. He used them well.

Mrs. P. was to be moved into the nursing home later on this day, Friday. On Saturday Jack arrived at the home, having scouted out the facility, he knew where all the exits were. With him was a nomadic preacher and a couple of Jack's roundworm friends. At her bedside Jack and Mrs. P were wed, chalkboard or not, her grunt, yes or no, was taken as an "I do." The certificated but unschooled preacher concluded his analysis of what had occurred that evening by intoning to all who would listen, "What a wonderful man, Jack, taking his beloved home to care for her."

"God does work wondrous things," the itinerant advised when he spoke later in a courtroom filled with enough interested people for a preacher of his ilk to see it as a congregation. "So does the Devil," I thought, considering Jack's malignity.

Following the bedside ceremony, Jack, Mrs. P's husband, at least for the moment, with the help of his crew, pushed the wheelchair from the nursing home room through exit doors to Jack's truck, and from this make-shift ambulance, to his apartment home. She was pushed across the threshold, and there she remained for as near as I could tell reconstructing the events, about 20 minutes.

No time for Malmsey. There was no celebration, no shivaree. She overwhelmed Jack. She had tubes protruding from her body that were meant to be attached to other tubes filled with medication he'd abandoned at the nursing home. He went through all his Kleenex and considerable toilet tissue just soaking up the mucous, which erupted periodically and served as her pitiful wedding veil.

It was horrible. The preacher and Jack's two friends had left the newlyweds as soon as Jack's place had been reached. "It seemed the right thing to do," the preacher later testified in his honeyed, mellifluous, and sanctimonious voice, seeing himself as an agent of God with an important role in this episode. "I left with the full knowledge that God will provide," he preached in recounting the event. Mrs. P. was put back into Jack's truck and transplanted to Penrose Hospital, the nearest place where she could be dumped off. "She's too much for me," Jack said; "she needs a doctor." He checked her into Penrose signing as her "husband" oblivious, I imagine, to what familial support obligations could result from such an admission.

She lived though this episode. That was surprising. Jack ignored her; he didn't even come to the hospital to see her. His scheme was completed. She was no longer needed. Her role now was to die. "Thank God for Medicare," he said, perhaps getting religion after what must have been his first round with a man purportedly of the cloth, after seeing the hospital bill I showed him, one he didn't have to pay. Medicare and the supplemental policy Mrs. P. owned did.

"I'm her husband," Jack repeated to me as often as he could. He'd been to a lawyer, discovered that as spouse he'd get all when she dies. Everything that she has would be his because she has no kids. He even referred to her resources as *"our"* stuff. Not all is lost, I thought, he wasn't yet claiming sole ownership. But he soon would be. I knew that. She didn't have long to live — even with what appeared now to be helpful care.

The marriage had to be annulled. It was a ruse, nonsense, nonconsensual, a scheme, contrived to secure an inheritance. Regardless of what Mrs. P's Will says, Jack, as surviving spouse, is entitled to receive a marital share. In this case that would be everything. And that must not happen.

A guardian was needed and a conservator, one other than Jack, a neutral fiduciary. And this must be done quickly. Emergency orders are needed. So we filed, alleging a fraudulent marriage, got a bank appointed as conservator; now her funds were temporarily safe, and a smart ad litem guardian was named, a sensitive lawyer who could act to annul the marriage on Mrs. P's behalf.

We looked for a really tough trial lawyer, one who would salivate when the facts of what occurred were related. Anyone could be picked. Mrs. P's exchequer could afford it — better her money be spent in this way than for Jack's pleasures. The temporary guardian was empowered to initiate the action — to determine whether the "marriage" was invalid and void *ab initio*. The lawyer-guardian empowered to initiate the hearing acted quickly, even got the matter advanced on the docket, avoided every delaying tactic that Jack's counsel advanced, because of Mrs. P's foreshortened life expectancy. The court made clear it had one issue before it — is this marriage valid or not?

It wasn't! That was the verdict. Medical staff, caring RNs from the Academy and aides, physicians, Penrose Hospital's emergency room staff, caregivers, all there to a person testifying that Mrs. P. could not verbalize I do or I don't. All grunts sounded the same. All attempted speech, even to save herself from this unwanted marriage produced the life—threatening mucous, muck that Mrs. P's body would not stop manufacturing.

Jack's preacher, even though colorful, was not helpful to Jack's defense, although having blessed the union, and having signed the license, he testified that he " . . . sure thought she said 'I do' or 'yes.' She was affirmative," he grimly said. And, he repeated what was his answer to all of life's mysteries again: "You know," he intoned, looking at the patient judge, "God does work wondrous things," whatever he meant by that. But he said it pontifically and with authority. He was convinced that the Almighty was somehow at work in all of this and that the result is "God's will." He seemed to enjoy his role. The witness box provided a modest pulpit and Theology 101 was frequently interjected in response to counsel's questions.

Mrs. P., of course, couldn't attend the trial, but her friends recounted the event to her. She raised her eyelids when the preacher's "God will provide," pronouncements were reported — not funny to Mrs. P., of course. She felt no providing when it came to her.

But when the verdict was read, Jack lost and walked, actually rushed, glumly out of the courtroom, but not far. Mrs. P.'s trial lawyers had the District Attorney there, too. The malignant act that made this trial necessary constituted criminal fraud. The DA followed Jack out of our local "Old Bailey" and I never saw Jack again.

I gained even more respect for our often maligned trial lawyer colleagues because of their exemplary conduct in handling this trial. I waited around to thank them. "Our pleasure," they said. "Send me your bill. I'll see that it's immediately paid." And I did. The day I got it I walked to the bank with a court order approved by her guardian, authorizing payment, and hand carried the cashier's check to my colleagues. I wanted to see these heroes and thank them again for Mrs. P. She knew about the trial. She knew she won. I went straight to her new safe home, the best nursing center in the city, and told her. She cried. "T Y," she wrote on the chalkboard. She was even more feeble now and it seemed to take forever for her to print those two letters. "Thank you" was it's message "for all you've done." I took the chalk from her. "You're worth it," I replied.

#

I read it in the obit column — seven days after the trial: Jack died! He died first! I was disbelieving, in shock. Did the trial do him in, or the DA — or his own malignity? Would he have died first anyway?

I headed to the nursing home to see Mrs. P. and to tell her what had apparently occurred. "Jack — dead," I said, using the abbreviated style that I had become accustomed to using when we "spoke," handing her the obituary. She read it slowly, and motioned for the chalkboard.

"G . . . " She struggled to form this letter, but that's as far as she needed to go. I knew the rest. I picked up the board and finished the sentence for her. "God does work wondrous things!"

She nodded from the first letter as I began to print. "I'm reading your mind. We must be spending too much time together," I teased, and I think I saw a smile, a difficult gesture for her. Her mouth was wiped. I squeezed her hand. It was time to leave. We both knew that this was also the final goodbye. She could now relax. Jack's trial was behind her. His scheme was not accomplished. She had her unerased chalkboard at her bedside to remind her of that.

Postscript

Elder abuse occurs in various ways. We see it commonly in business promotions. Sales of magazine subscriptions (*see* "You May Already Be A Winner") is only one way insidious marketing agents take advantage of the deteriorating minds of elders whom they craftily solicit.

Caregivers, too, those employed to work in the elders' homes, promote themselves as needful, as deserving of aid, and ingenuously become recipients of both *inter vivos* gifts, those made while the elder is living, and as devisees, beneficiaries under Wills with the largess they covet received when their fragile employer dies. (*See* the author's article, "Contracts to Devise or Gift Property — Latent and Insidious Abuse of Older Persons," *Probate Law Jo.*, Boston, Mass., vol. 12, No. 1, 1994.)

Abusers ingratiate themselves to their intended victims (illustrated in "Think of Me as the Daughter You Never Had"), and may surreptitiously victimize their increasingly febrile patsies, (illustrated in "...Wondrous Things").

Lawyers working with older clients are aware that children may be the worst abusers in our community of elders, insisting on their inheritance now when they "need" it, encouraging gifting from their parents so all the wealth, however meager, won't be lost on their parents' possible long-term nursing home care.

Recognized or not, parents' values typically include wanting to leave something of their estate, however pitifully small it may be, to their children. It represents the parents' social immortality. The fear of nursing home costs consuming all of their savings fuels the intensity of the decision.

"Give it to me now or spend it on nursing home costs," spit out in an acrid tone and manner by self-interested children and other hangers-on, is a dichotomy the elders then face. Many make the transfers, gifts that result in the donors' own poverty, an event that without subtlety, suggests to them that their lives are over. When they enter the confines of the nursing home, which thereafter follows, Medicaid is relied on, an embarrassment to many donor-parents. They saved their earnings for an end-life filled with fun, their lives lived out in their own homes, options now taken away by their self-interested issue or others, "friends" who take advantage of their relationship, abuse which satisfies the donees' own greed.

PART THREE

*"Is My Bed Still There?"**

It's been a number of years, now, perhaps 20, since my family and I were served by a remarkable civil servant. Our postman introduced himself when we moved into his territory. We were Clif & Carolyn to him. He was Harold to us. He knew our young children, our cats and our collie, Duke. He would carefully watch for our big dog when he drove down our street, knowing that Duke patrolled the property, and would be gleefully running around the postal truck as it approached and before it stopped. Duke knew that the truck carried our friend, his friend, too, and neither grew tired of participating in this daily exercise.

While mail carriers since Harold's retirement have come and gone from the route that takes them past our home, it is this one person in this role that our family fondly remembers.

Recently, a thin and fragile lady, elegantly dressed, her short silver gray hair stylishly coiffured, came to our office accompanied by her two daughters. "We had to put Harold in a home," she said. "He became too ill for me to handle. You know him," said his still perky and pretty wife. "He was your postman."

"How is he doing there?" I asked.

"OK."

"OK?"

"Well, not too well. But there's no way that he can be cared for at home."

She wiped away a tear. You could sense the sorrow she felt because, lively as she was, she could no longer both medicate and physically care for her once sturdy but now fragile and age-enfeebled husband.

"When I wake up," she continued, "my pillow is wet. I must cry in the night. But in

* This chapter is endnoted. The notes can be found at the end of this chapter.

the day, I'm strong."

"You feel that you shouldn't cry?" There is no response.

"It's healthful to cry — and you can cry here."

Then a daughter interjects — there is discomfort in Mom crying or needing to cry —

"I saw Dad this morning. He asked, 'Is my bed still there?'"

"What did he mean?" I responded.

We didn't discuss the metaphor, but isn't this imagery uncamouflaged, a euphemism palliative to the soul of the ill and aging patient, and perhaps to those who love him as well?[1]

Am I going home someday?

I haven't given up. Has your mother?

#

If my bed is still there, then there is still reason to hope. The possibility, however remote, to return home if only to die there is not excised.

We deal with sadness in our practices.* Our clients in the context that this essay addresses are depressed. They are afraid. They may be angry. They are looking for relief.

In their end-life homes they are demeaned — called by their first names by persons whom they don't know and don't care to know. They're told what to do and when to do it. The calls for help among some echo in the nursing home hallways and are unceasingly shrill, and pathetically unanswered. And no Ombudsman can work the miracle that patients hope for — a cure of the elders' frailty — a return to their earlier history, to their homes and to a fun life that they fantasize experiencing again.

These coffin-ships are not home. Our clients' steerage is unwanted. The destination is reached for each of these passengers as each dies. The ships are charted to accomplish this. This is their purpose, to hold not to cure; to confine — to make possible physical comfort-care when it is nowhere else, for whatever reason, available.

The elders' feelings, however aware of their environment as they may still be, are distressingly ignored. They are sometimes thoughtlessly treated as the breathing dead. One nursing home in the city where I live, for example, is depressingly situate across the street from the city's large cemetery, perhaps 100 feet, a stone's short throw to the nearest grave marker. This setting, in bitter allegory, is reminiscent of a 13th century poet's Inferno.[2] It is signage, the Dantean neon across from the nursing institution's entrance, announcing the hopeless future of those who enter.

#

* This story was originally written and published for lawyers practicing elder-law and therefore the plural pronoun "we" or "us" refers to these legal specialists, and acknowledges the reality that conferences with elders and their families will often be difficult because of an unwanted but anticipated soon-to-arrive demise.

Among the first books that I bought as a young lawyer was one entitled *The Successful Practice of Law*. I had taken the train to Denver from my home in Topeka, Kansas, to sit for the Colorado Bar exam, a grueling four-day affair — and on my return from Colorado to Kansas I planned to read — and did read this book. I wasn't altogether confident that I would be able to apply its teachings. Four months had to pass before I would learn whether or not my law school J.D. would be accompanied by a Colorado law license.

The rather thick text of the *Success* book didn't have a chapter on elder law. There was no mention of nursing homes or even a suggestion that a client would ever be seen other than in the serenity of the lawyer's own suite. I'm not sure now what the author meant by the word "successful" in the book's title, but I regretfully suspect that its emphasis was one of lawyer prosperity and lawyer self-interest.[3]

Success for us and for all conscientious lawyers is, of course, making a positive difference in the lives of those who ask us for help. And this means that we enter into the Dantean cahvs[4] where our clients reside, and while there listen, not lecture; if only by our presence and the hardware that we carry[5] we affirm that we care. We hold the thin skeletal hands of those whom we are called to comfort, and in this posture we feel each palpitation of our clients' weary and burdened hearts. We are affected, too, by the " . . . emotions exposed by the imminence of their deaths."[6]

This urging to make the lives of elders more joyful with no theological purpose is a call from humanity to us as lawyers who intend to make a positive difference in the lives of others. Our humanism,[7] notwithstanding our individual metaphysical tastes, separates us from not only rascally pettifoggers, but other "successful" lawyers, however defined, as well.

ENDNOTES TO "IS MY BED STILL THERE?"

1. *See* Theodor Reik, *Listening With the Third Ear*, Grove Press, N.Y. (1948). A similar euphemism, and one that is perhaps more obvious, was spoken by an elder who, looking at her new coat, sadly said to her family, "This is my last coat."
2. Dante Alighier, 1265-1321, *Divine Comedy*, iii.1. "Abandon all hope, you who enter," inscription at the entrance to hell.
3. "Successful" is defined as prosperous, having wealth or status or both. *The Concise Oxford Dictionary of Current English*, Clarendon Press, Oxford (1995), p. 1391; "success," while defined as the attainment of wealth, is more broadly defined to include the accomplishment of a goal; a favorable outcome, p. 1391. *The Oxford Universal Dictionary*, Clarendon Press, Oxford 1955), p.2066, also distinguishes between these two words, with "successful" related to "that [which] attains to wealth or position ...." Success is defined, as it is above, far more broadly. The noun is from Latin, successus. Its use as a term evidencing the satisfaction of a goal is first recorded in 1586. R. Barnhart, *Dictionary of Etymology*, Harper (1995), p. 774. There is no reference to the word successful in the etymology text. Succeed (Lt. *succedere*) was first used to indicate a favorable result, used in Middle English, after 1475, a century earlier, and is more akin to the modern use of the term successful. Id.
4. Cave, pronounced cahv, Fr. for cellar. *See The Concise Oxford Dictionary of Current English, id.*, p. 340. Caves (long vowel) from Lt. cava, (p. cavus) meaning hollow (places); in France caves are underground storage places. They are hollow places. "Holh cave" is the term for such hollows in Old English. The container metaphor is not an inappropriate description of what for many is their last home. It is a hollow place where existential self—determination ends.
5. The hardware we carry includes Advance Directives, our clients' Wills, Funeral Directives and Tangible Property Memorandums, among other legal documents.
6. Walter Goodman, "The Art of Making Life Easier as It Nears an End," *The New York Times*, (March 18, 1996), p. B-3.
7. By humanism is meant a concern for and an appreciation of human values and human capabilities. The term arose during the Renaissance (1350-1650) at a time when the emphasis was on secular studies and Medieval religious authority was being rejected. Modernly, humanism emphasizes the virtue and importance of human values and respect for scientific knowledge. *See The Concise Columbia Encyclopedia Third Edition*, Columbia University Press, N.Y., (1994), p. 404.

*Hisssss**

"You have a client here who insists on seeing you."

The call came from an employee of one of the city's large nursing homes, and the language and tone sounded of irritation.

Heather, a long-time client, widowed ten years, had arrived at Patientrest earlier on the day of the call, transported from Penrose, one of our city's large hospitals. My client had fallen at her home and needed some repair. The hospital visit was to be followed by a month at a sprawling one-story nursing home in the city, housing 100 or so elders. It is no Eden.[1]

I found Heather in a two-patient room lying on a bed with no side-rails. "I'm afraid that I'm going to fall out," were her first words to me, even before she said hello. No timbre in her voice, it was strained and harsh, and came from a tense, dry, and unsonorous throat.

Rigid, both hands clinging to the cot-like bedsides, eyes tightly closed, Heather's phantasm had placed her on the highest bench of an enormous Ferris wheel with her seat suspended on the amusement's outer edge. The rotation had stopped, but her bench was perceived as swinging with any movement she made — and with the front protective bar missing. She was fettered, and her cries for help to be freed from this captivity, disregarded by the unpitying, obdurate staff were votaries without hope. She had been this way since her transport to the rest home several hours earlier, before I arrived. She was febrile from her anxiety and couldn't move, even to taste the meal that had been brought to her and later removed by uncaring, faineant workers. Her daylong cries for comfort were ignored, blending in, I suppose, with those of others. No Halcyon[2] days here — for anyone.

A decade ago, following her banker-husband's death, Heather executed durable agencies for both medical and financial decision-making, naming her lawyer as her agent. "My daughter is ill and my son is in Columbia," she explained, expressed in a manner that the city, too, sounded like a disease. That distant, he could be of little help to her.

Over the next decade, perhaps annually, responding to her calls, I drove over to the simple and pretty white cottage where Heather lived. It was located on a quiet side street, near our community's large hospital, in the city's north end. The homes there, filled with long-time residents of the city, are not regimented, similar in style nor

* This chapter is endnoted. The notes can be found at the end of this chapter.

unpleasantly close together. The yards, including Heather's, are neat, filled with flowers and in spring and summer with trimmed green grass. The north-end side-street community is obviously proud of its quarters in the city and keeps its habitat tidy. Even after her husband's death and the consequential shrinkage of her monthly income, Heather never complained about the obvious cost that obeisance to the small community's values required.

On each of these visits to Heather's home I toured the house and revisited the hideaways where all of her important papers were stashed, identified by drawers in dressers and desks. I knew where the small, portable safebox was hidden, and told about the cache it held. The locations of Heather's private horde, all secreted in an unused tidy and petite back bedroom located in her small home never changed, and after the first of my several visits, I could have led the tour.

"You need to go to the house," Heather spoke on the day following her entry into the nursing home. "The tax papers need to be delivered to Gene." Gene was her accountant. "Center drawer — desk," I responded, showing off my memory. "No," she whispered. "I've moved them." They had been divided and were now to be found in three places: the dresser, center drawers one and two, and in a metal filing box, hidden in the closet. Ten years of memorizing where each important paper was placed, and, of course, she had moved them. "My safe," she continued. "Do you remember where it is?" "Yes," I answered, assuming that she hadn't moved that as well, but when my legal assistant, Sheila, and I went to the house later that day, the portable safe was nowhere to be found. If it is still there, in the home, she hid it well. The key, of course, remained in its hiding place, a covered porcelain dish on the dresser, eight feet away from its host-closet in which the portable safe, a locked, old fishing tackle box, at one time, at least, had been hidden.

My conversation with Heather was interrupted by a loudspeaker installed in the home's large great room located not far (enough) from Heather's quarters. "Okay, okay," a voice spoke, but, regrettably, not until the neolithic speaker had first blown into the microphone creating an eardrum-splitting screech. She had to be sure that the system was on high volume. It was.

"Okay, okay," she again announced. "What kind of a sound does a pig make?" I could hear a few "oink, oinks," from a brigade of couldn't-care-less patients strapped into wheelchairs, left helplessly to fend for themselves by callous aides who had abandoned their charges perhaps to steal a quick smoke while the degrading, puerile "entertainment" progressed. In order, the prosaic sounds of cows were next, followed by just about every farm animal that I ever want to hear again. I was hoping that the entertainer of the day, a volunteer from the outside who seemed enraptured by her own noisy tosh, would ask for the sound of a snake. Heather and I would have joined in, but no such luck, no hissing on this day.

I shut the door to my client's small room. Heather and I had heard enough. "You've got to get me out of here," she said. "Indeed," was my response. This cannot be her place of exile because her journey's end is near.

I was given other instructions and with marching orders she'd given, kissed her lightly on her forehead, and left. On the previous day, the date of her admittance to Patientrest, I had arranged for her being moved from her bed to a large overstuffed chair in her room, and she seemed settled. I told the nurse that she was not to be replaced in bed because of the great panic she experienced. Now relaxed in the overstuffed, no longer spinning and holding on to her bed's edges, after I left she made her way with her walker to the administrator's office, and I learned, told the *chargé d'affaires* there that this is why her lawyer had shown up that day — and she'd better have the side-rail model when he reappeared — or else.

The following day I returned to report on my progress. I had the checklist with all important matters accomplished: "Call my son, deposit my checks; open a trust account, pay the bills ..." Pretty impressed with my own efficiency, I expected high praise. But Heather seemed disinterested. She wasn't listening. She remained passive in her new hospital-style bed. She was obviously depressed. Her ankles were swollen and were weeping fluids — a sign, I'm told, of congestive heart failure.

I quietly held Heather's hand. We said nothing for several minutes. "My birthday was the 31st," she finally blurted out, "about a month ago." A few seconds passed; "I'm eighty-five." I nodded. There was more coming, and I didn't want to distract her or reply with impertinence — best to say nothing, wait her out. It's still her turn to speak — mine to listen.

"My mother died when she was eighty-five." As she spoke, Heather was looking into my eyes — to see my reaction. Her own eyes were tearing and rheumy.

"And . . ?" I quietly said, recognizing the parallel, asking her in this way to continue.

"That's why I'm depressed."[3]

Well, I could certainly understand that. Heather loved her mother, and does the bonding between mother and daughter, when for fortunate daughters it does attach, ever end? Their birthdays were near in time, celebrated together. Heather wore her mother's jewelry, and had her mother's picture framed and prominently displayed in her home on a wall near the chair where Heather sat and read and although her mother's death occurred many years ago, was still a fresh, discalming memory. And now Heather is alone, her children far removed from her, one by schizophrenic illness, the other by distance and what his mother perceives as disinterest. And now the comfort of her home is being taken away by Heather's own discrepitude. These separations in her life — from her mother, her husband, her two children, and now her home, are not easily accommodated, and her desiderate anxiety understandable, but there is no quick anodyne for her disquieting emotions. Her helplessness and mine is accompanied by the contumely and ceaseless background of shrill, discordant, and pitiful human imitations of sounds that animals make.... This is an unquiet sepulcher, an unwanted asylum, a noisy human warehouse without vomitory.

#

Heather was tiring. Her eyes now closing. An aide arrived and tucked her into bed — side rails up — a nap before dinner. She had the late seating, 6:30, so she could dose a bit, hopefully to feel refreshed upon awakening.

The animal sound-show had mercifully stopped and dutiful aides were moving the wheelchair-imprisoned audience back to their rooms to prepare for their evening meal. I walked through the area where the noisy comedian had been. She, too, was now gone, headed perhaps to another sanctuary to inflict her aggravating nonsense on yet another assembly of unwilling participants. This is an unfriendly place, a depressing shelter, I thought. Unsmiling, unfriendly aides, no animals, no birds, no vegetation, only faded skeletal plants, dusty and ugly, made from repugnant, hollow plastic, seated here and there within the warehouse hallways. This is a grim tomb in which human beings are being stored, abused by nonsense, hounded by the unceasing moans of those nearing repose. It is not a restful place, this entrance to death for those forced to suffer here.

I reached the exit door, turned and looked around. What sound does a snake make — the only voice I believe which the entertainer ignored. I took a deep breath. No one was around.... I hissed.

ENDNOTES TO HISSSSS

1. See Wm. H. Thomas, M.D., *Life Worth Living (How Someone You Love Can Still Enjoy Life in a Nursing Home)*, VanderWyk & Burnham Publishers, (1996).
2. Halcyon was a mythological bird, thought in antiquity to breed in a nest floating at sea in the Winter solstice, charming the wind and waves into calm.
3. Not uncommon, birth anniversaries announce the increasing nearness of our own mortality. "On May 23, the day before [Justice] Cardozo's sixty-eighth birthday, [a friend] paid [him] a visit, but no one was permitted to see him after that because as Rauh [one of his law clerks] explained, 'he has become so highly emotional — partly over his birthday — that visitors evoke tears and sadness generally.'" Richard Polenberg, *The World of Benjamin Cardozo*, Harvard Univ. Pr

"For Awhile I Guess I Was Dead"

Irma lost her husband after nearly six decades of marriage. She arranged for his burial, and bought two grave sites and an eolith-like stone on which his name and hers were carved. Their respective birth dates were shown, and his was to evince his date of death as well.

It was difficult for Irma to visit the memorial garden in which her familial companion was now buried, but one day several months after his entombment, she did. And there neatly inscribed on the stone was the year of death, just as she had ordered: 1913-1998 — but the carved-on date was beside her name, not his!

An embarrassed stone cutter took care of the error moments after Irma's frantic call. The problem was solved, and Irma was telling me about it. The stonecutter had been graciously forgiven. "For awhile I guess I was dead," she reasoned. She sounded serious, and I was too timid to invite further discourse on this theme.

Irma's home is a small apartment on the eighth floor of a high-rise in our city. Her living room faces west and from this vista she can see her mountains, the Rockies. "Stylishly rococo," is her description of them. Stylishly rococo, indeed! They stream by her balcony decorating her Western horizon as far north and south as she can see. At an earlier time Irma and her mate had often picnicked among these granite peaks, but that was long ago. Irma, now, only imagines their wildflower meadows and their clear as crystal high mountain streams, but that's enough; she accepts the limitations that age introduces to us all. In the Fall she can still see large yellow puncta, dots of color from the Rockies' Aspened forests. And she never tires of viewing their grandiose peaks, some tipped with snow most of the year.

#

"I keep falling," Irma admitted. "I think I stumble over my rug edges." She paused. "And I fell in the bath, too." Following a long introduction, admiring her unique view of our earth's great art, the purpose of this day's meeting was disclosed. "I've lost my husband. Am I to lose my home as well?"

Irma fell in the bath. No rugs there. She's declining — and she knows it. This is why I was called by Irma — not about the error on the tombstones; that, she had repaired, but the death date is eerily metaphoric, certainly disturbing because she must now be considering the reality of the end of her life.

I looked into her eyes, magnified by her thick-lens glasses. Her eyes were tearing. She spoke in quick, short staccato-like sentences, accentuating the emotion: "This is my home. I can't leave. You've got to help me. The manager knows you're coming. She told me I have to leave because I keep falling. I told her that she'd have to deal with my lawyer!" She spoke this final sentence with emphasis.

"Where is John Wayne when I need him?" I thought. I imagined the big guy, all 6'6", coming through a Western bar's swinging doors, hatted with a dirty but one time white wide-brim nearly touching the transom, six-shooters on both hips, a grim "don't mess with me," demeanor emphasized with narrowed eyes and compelling frown. I imagined the visigoths scrambling, getting out of his way. But I knew the landlady here at Mountainview. She's taller than I, and tougher — not about to run from me or anyone, except, perhaps the cowboy.

This is a critical moment in the life of my 89-year-old client. For her leaving her home, forced to leave, is like death itself, the end of her life. And she faces this alone now, without her life's mate.

#

"Why weren't you here this morning?"

This was the greeting I received recently from a remarkable sculptor, an artist who was facing the end of his life's work. Surrounded by his magnificent art, in coveralls stained with the residue of the media in which he worked, the grime that steel leaves in the process of molding it into dramatic, mobile sculpture. He was sullen, scowling as he spoke.

"I never come by in the morning. Didn't I tell you I'd stop by after work? That's when I always come — about 6:00 o'clock. It's 6:00 now."

He didn't answer, morose, troubled by the woeful spirits that ruled his mind and body. He was nearing his fourscore and ten, the time when he would be accompanied from his home, too. He had outlived the energy he needs to maintain his large, beautifully ornate self-crafted home, and the strength required to continue creating his grand art. His life as a sculptor is ending, and he is in despair. He ambled to his workshop studio; I followed. He shook his head, paced about the room, angry at the gods, his fate, his woe. He talked, raved really. I listened, but his anguish was not quieted. As 7:00 o'clock approached, I readied to leave, and we walked through his workshop, towards its exit that led into the roadway. He stopped by a large anvil mounted near the doorway. "Good-bye, my good friend," I voiced. He was silent. I drove down the foothills roadway, and perhaps the engine noise of my old Subaru muffled the sound of the .38, but its missile ended the life of my friend. Someone heard it, though, and a call was waiting for me as I edged into my home's driveway. It was the coroner. I headed back, met with the police, told them what I knew, and tried to comfort my friend's wife who arrived at the home shortly after I'd first left. She met the police there and was shown his corpse by them. His body was slumped on the concrete floor where we had said our final good-bye — mine vocal, his said in silence, and then, after I departed, with the sound a gun makes.

"Hi, Pat." I'd knocked on the manager's office door, the tough one I'd met before, the one who'd just told Irma she'd have to move.

"Where can I take Irma, Pat?" I asked. "She says she's got to leave."

"She falls all the time."

"That's what she tells me." She said you'd been wonderful to her, and check on her every day, eight floors up on a slow elevator. 'I wouldn't be alive today without Pat,' she told me," careful not to overdo the praise. "Any idea why she's falling?"

"It could be the rugs."

"Really?" I answered, quite surprised by this response. "Her toes might get caught under the edges," she offered, sounding to me like she's working on a solution.

"Would she let us take them up, so she'd just have the hardwood?"

"I'll ask her," Pat replied.

What's all this talk about having to move, I wondered. Irma's imagination? Wanting attention? Is it a way to get a sympathetic visit from her lawyer? The subject of Irma's having to move to a safer site, whatever that might be, was never suggested in my conversation with the building's "tough" manager. This announcement came only from Irma, perhaps a verbalization of her fear — anticipation of what she fears Pat may one day have to say.

Irma experienced several falls resulting in bruises but no breaks, even after the rugs were taken up, so she must have strong bones. In one incident she struck her head on the floor and told me that she felt like someone was in the room with her hitting her cranium with a baseball bat; so she was hurting. But she recovered from this and the other falls also. She dutifully used her lifeline, the alert for Pat, the tough landlady, so she could be rescued, and, in addition, Pat unfailingly and cheerfully stops by Irma's place several times a day to check on what has become her charge, and now her special friend. Irma knows she's coming and leaves her door open for easy entry. Knowing each other for many years as, respectively, apartment manager and resident, they've now bonded, and care for each other.

For now, Irma's problem is solved. She falls but she gets up and if she can't, she has her lifeline. And "isn't this better," she asks, "than living in the 'dying place'," the nursing home she dreads. Irma has stashed much of her wealth. She knows that she can get twenty-four hour care in her small home, eight floors up with a mountain view, when the time comes — if it does — when she'll need this. She also knows that her bed can be moved in by the window if full bed rest is needed, so she can continue to look out at her mountains, watch their seasons, and still be moved by the inspiration which their beauty brings to her. Pat has confirmed this. It's a promise made possible by this new friendship. Pat is Irma's defender. For them, now, there will be no goodbye.

Postscript

"I don't believe in nursing homes," a client recently reported in response to my suggestion that he purchase long term care insurance for his fiancè. His net worth was near one million, hers $85,000 dollars, valued optimistically. I explained to him that once married, he'd be responsible to pay for her nursing home care if long term care was needed.

We parried for nearly a full hour. He left frustrated and I'll never see him again. Ignoring the government view that his soon-to-be wife and he are treated as one economic unit when long term care aid is applied for, his remaining options will be to pay her nursing home care bill, which he indicated he had no intention of doing, or divorcing her, which would be tragic because there is mutual love in their relationship and each does care, I'm convinced, for the other.

No one "believes" in nursing homes. Their necessity is ignored. None of us intend ever to live — and die — in one. But even Irma isn't safe. ("For Awhile I Guess I was Dead"). Commitments change. If 24 hour care is needed at $15.00 per hour, that's $131,400 a year, enough to soon exhaust the personal exchequer of most readers.

But lawyers who work with elder clients face the nursing home reality daily. Visits are made to see clients who now live in these homes. Advance health care directives are written and signed there, so are Wills and Trusts and whatever else comes through the lawyer's office that requires the competent but physically incapacitated client's signature.

Not all of the nursing home centers are exemplary. In fact, staffed with minimum wage and often not well educated aides, we no doubt expect more care from the staff in such homes than our clients and their families receive. Walking into such an institution to see one who "doesn't believe in them," but is now there, sitting in a bean bag chair — a mischievous physical restraint — in his own urine, remains indelible, and we cannot forget witnessing the demeaning moment, and forgiving the home's overworked aide in charge of this cell is difficult as well. It's no wonder that we want to be in our own bed and in our own home, and the reality that our bed may not now be there, metaphoric or not, as we languish in some form of assisted living, is surely dementing.

Death may be viewed eagerly by some in the assembly of needful care home residents, and suicide, where physical ability allows, surely, does not go unconsidered. These issues elder law attorneys and readers consider in the stories that make up Part Three of *Selma's Cat*.

PART FOUR

*Come let us kiss and part**[1]

"For my part, in truth, I would rather be old less long than be old before I am old."[2]

#

Some of our clients are waiting for death — ready, more than ready — angry when they awake because another day must unfold for them. They are energyless, without hope, their depression poorly masked.

#

. . . [M]any a time
I have been half in love with easeful Death,
Call'd him soft names in many a mused rhyme,
To take into the air my quiet breath;
Now more than ever seems it rich to die,
To cease upon the midnight with no pain, . . .[3]

#

"I hate for you to see me this way."

"What way?"

"Like I am now. I should be dead."

She spoke with a slurred speech and haltingly, the unwanted souvenir of an earlier stroke. "I want to die. I'm 92. I can no longer paint or write; I can't move my fingers to sign my name."

Healthy in her earlier years, Lillian is now skeletal and very frail. She can't walk unaided. Her speech sometimes requires her husband's interpretation when she attempts to form words.

My client is an artist, a PenWoman, one of only six having published in three art-

* This chapter is endnoted. Michael Drayton, John Keats, and the Bard are featured, illustrating the emotions affecting elders nearing end life. The notes can be found at the end of this chapter.

forms, writings, including poetry, music and art. She has painted in both oil and watercolor, Chinese brush, and pen and ink. Mightily creative, she.

She was reading, (or attempting to read) when I arrived, seated comfortably on her couch, cozy, in one of its corners with her feet drawn up beneath her, a pretty pink house slipper poking out from under her long robe. Beside her was an old, inch-thick book, its pages now browning and its cover faded. Harold Bell Wright was its author. *The Eyes of the World*, a 1914 novel, is no longer in print, originally published in New York by John Wanamaker. Her copy is a reprint.

"She sleeps and reads and rereads her book; that's all she does now," her husband of 94 said. He appeared to be remarkably healthy and was stylish in appearance — polished pennyloafers, longish grey hair swept horizontally from front to back, only slightly messed when he ran his hands through it, which he did from time to time as he spoke. "I've read it, too, six times." The book looked well read. Little did its author know how important it would be to my friends, now in their decline. It gave them, and especially Lillian, something to look forward to when she awoke, a book, imagined perhaps, about her life. She assumed the role of its heroine, an artist, a creator like herself. For her it was a sustaining almost-biography.

She and her husband, called Penni by her through their 70 years of marriage, now live in a small apartment, a condominium, not owned, a rental for them. A large, unpolished solid walnut desk divides the large studio into a living room and what was once a dining area. Now unused, the dining room houses miscellaneous things. Her room, where she once spent wondrous hours painting and rhyming and writing, I wasn't invited to see. "Too messy," Penni said. I didn't venture into the single bedroom either. Their quarters are small.

Before I arrived I imagined that there would be many paintings framed on the walls of Lillian's home. "There all up," Penni said, when I asked about what I imagined might be a cache of painting treasures lining the apartment's walls. I counted perhaps 20 — nothing grand. All of her great works had been sold, many with their juried ribbons attached. One endearing water color image was of a young girl profiled against a wind that caused her chestnut hair to flow behind her as she stood in a field of tall grass, her soft red-colored skirt only slightly hidden by the growing hay. She held wild flowers in cupped hands. Her impressionist features suggested youthful innocence, sweetness, a memory, perhaps, for Lillian, its artist, of a happy memory in her own youth. The subdued shaded watercolor had appeared on the cover of PenWomen, and I had seen it there, 20 years ago or so. The positive impression it made on me remained. I blurted out, "Jenny," it's title. Lillian may have been pleased, I don't know. She couldn't smile, having little control of the muscles that allow curvature of our lips upward when our emotions are pleasant ones, when we are happy. This response of her body had been stilled — but I spotted happiness in her greying eyes.

The longish prelude was nearing its end. I was called to Lillian's and Penni's home "to go over our affairs." That phase of the interview began when I reseated myself in front of the couch on a straight chair that I strategically moved there for a purpose. I ignored the low and comfortable overstuffed model I suspect was intended for me. But now I was close enough to touch Lillian. I could hold her hand.

We looked at their wills and durable agencies. Hers were fine and his, too, really, but because I would be acting as fiduciary for them — "our son is too far away and too busy," — I suggested minor changes, ones that obligated me to consult with their son and to keep him informed, provisions that could give his parents comfort, and protection for me. We left Lillian as Penni's primary fiduciary, agent and executrix. This was notice to her that her dignity and rightful place in decision-making would not be usurped.

Bank accounts were described — account numbers and institutions — almost a half million described by Penni as "the pittance" that remained. "Some pittance," I exclaimed! Talking to a lawyer who was presumed by him to be wealthy, he needed confirmation that he had done well, that Lillian could continue to be provided for. And he received that assurance. "Well done," I said, and I meant it. Suddenly, certainly without warning, Penni, looking at me with intense seriousness, blurted out, even calling me by my last name — "Mr. Kruse," — so I knew what was to follow would be serious, "what are your thoughts on suicide?"

#

My heart aches and a drowsy numbness pains
My sense, as though of Hemlock I had drunk,
Or emptied some dull opiate to the drains.
One minute past and Lethe—wards had sunk . . . .
That I might drink, and leave the world unseen,
And with thee fade away . . .[4]

#

"What are your thoughts on suicide?" That was Penni's (and I presumed,) Lillian's next question. New subject, the reason I was called. Ninety minutes had passed. It took that long to feel assurance that such a question could be asked.

#

No, no, go not to Lethe,[5] neither twist
  Wolf's bane,[6] tight-rooted for its poisonous wine;[7]
Nor suffer thy pale forehead to be kissed
  By nightshade,[8] ruby grape of Proserpine;[9]
Make not your rosary of yew-berries,

Nor let the beetle, nor the death-moth be
Your mournful Psyche,[10] nor the downy owl
A Partner in your sorrow's mysteries;
For shade to shade will come too drowsily
And drown the wakeful anguish of the soul.[11]

#

Lillian interjected, "Penni has such a good memory," she said, a seemingly unrelated comment. "He's 94," she went on . . . . I held her hand. I looked just at her. She was changing the subject. "What do you think about suicide," was not her question.

"This is my book," she continued — again, the wonderful book. Her history, her creative contributions, her fantasy, her life visualized on browning, faded pages.

Artists, poets, writers take us beyond our little villages, our small and insulated worlds, and give us joy and warmth and feeling. They enable us to see, to imagine a not thought-about reality. They give us vision and inspiration. They take the sameness and drabness from our lives. They stimulate our imagination and make our lives worth living. And we suddenly feel and know this as we are forced to look at the poverty and awfulness of areas in our world where war has disassembled people. The black and white, uncolored devastation of the human spirit seen in the emaciation and colorless hollow eyes of villagers representing worlds without health care, without food, without clothing, without dignity, without esteem, and surely, without poetry and literature and art, as well.

Lillian had made life better for those in her village, those fortunate enough to have read her writings, felt the effect of her poetry, and experienced the result of her imagination that her paints and palette made possible. And she knew that — and she knew it now.

This is my book — my life, and for Lillian it is not over and that was her unverbalized message to Penni, wasn't it? Penni — think about our memories, our 70 years together. Read the book. It's about our life, my art, your support. Don't give up on me now. Subsist on our joys. Our life is different; it's not like it was. But it's our life . . . . It's part of *our* book.

I smiled at Lillian. Wordless, it meant I understood, that I agreed. Life has not ended for you — and Penni's role has not ended in your life together either. His memories are good — and he just needed to be reminded of that and has been, by your timely, quiet eloquence. Of course, it wasn't my thoughts on suicide that Penni wished to hear anyway. He needed to think through his own feelings — bounce them off a trusted friend, and, more importantly, see what Lillian would think.

I looked at him. He had been quietly listening to his wife. Her words did not need embellishment for him, nor interpretation for the lawyer who was listening, who was part of this touching scene.

Love, which in spite of darkness
brought us hither,
Should in despite of light
keep us together . . . [12]

#

There was quiet for a long moment. There'll be no more talk of suicide — Penni got that message. He looked at his wife, frail, but not greatly depressed, different now, but accommodated to her condition, and still filled with inner dignity. "That time of year though mayst in me behold

When yellow leaves, or none, or few, do hang
Upon those boughs which shake against the cold,
Bare ruined choirs where late the sweet birds sang.
In me thou see'st the twilight of such day . . .
Death's second self, that seals up all the rest." [13]

#

"I'm glad," Penni finally spoke, knowing that he had come close,[14] "that Dr. Kevorkian isn't here, isn't in Colorado."

So am I.

ENDNOTES TO COME LET US KISS AND PART

1. "Since there is no [hope], come let us kiss and part." Michael Drayton (1563-1631). The actual metrical unit reads: "Since there's no help, come let us kiss and part."
2. Michel de Montaigne, "Of Books," quoting Brutus, *The Complete Essays*, Trans. and Edited by M. A. Screech (Penguin 1987), pp. 457, 466. Quoted by Montaigne in Latin, "Ego vero me minus diu senem esse mallem, quam esse senem antequam essem." Brutus was a highly respected statesman — 85-42 BCE, and helped lead the assassination plot against Caesar. Montaigne saw him as a skillful orator.
3. John Keats, a portion of "Ode to a Nightingale," a beautiful songed night bird to whom Keats speaks in §VI. The speaker is longing to die to the accompaniment of this beautiful singing bird. The opening phrase, omitted in this essay, begins, "Darkling [in the dark of night] I listen; and many a time . . . . " The final stanzas address the night bird. Also omitted, they continue, "While thou art pouring forth thy soul abroad, In such an ecstacy! Still wouldst thou sing, and I have ears in vain — To thy high requiem become a sod."
4. Id. A graveyard poem, Keats is saying in §§ I. and II., if only I could have a drink which would make me as free as you [the nightingale] and allow me entrance into the new world by the river (Lethe) of forgetfulness. Use of Lethe-"wards" in the Ode indicates a place or destination.
5. The river of forgetfulness, entrance to the new world.
6. Wolf's bane, a poisonous plant.
7. Don't kill yourself because of melancholy.
8. A black or red berried poisonous plant.
9. Also Proserpina, for Persephone, in Greek and Roman mythology, goddess of fertility, queen of the underworld, daughter of Zeus and Demeter. Her eight month return to earth annually symbolized the vegetative cycle. When she returned to Hades, earth's vegetation withered. *See Concise Columbia Encyclopedia*, (third ed.), Columbia Press (1994), p. 678.
10. *Supra* n.7.
11. John Keats, "Ode on Melancholy." Melancholy is pictured as a beautiful woman in drab garments in Greek mythology. An ode is a lyric poem in the form of an address, sung in Greek times, intimate, written in Latin by Horace and later day poets, including Keats.
12. John Donne, "Break of Day."
13. Wm. Shakespeare (1564-1616), Sonnnet 73. Shakespeare observes the approach of death, the Fall of our years, in this sonnet.
14. *Supra* n.1. There is no need to think of Drayton; no need to kiss and part; no justification to terminate the memories; no right to abandon another.

*Carrie**

He's now age 92, fully blind in one eye, and has little use of the other, the one he calls "my good eye." Glaucoma has taken away his sight, and he now moves about in a shadowy, indistinct world. But he doesn't complain. His spirit is his hopeful and optimistic companion. He continues his writing, and at age 91, published his second volume of poetry. It was the subject of a recent Paul Harvey news broadcast — it's that good.

Widowed, he's approaching his third year of separation from his muse, his inspiring goddess to whom he was married for 65 years. She remains his inspiration, and he quietly continues to grieve from this ectomy, recently penning these lines:

#

He sent me white roses
For happiness fled,
Pure white-petalled roses —
Our young love is dead.

Once red were the roses
He sent, loving me:
Pure red-petalled roses
He sent lovingly.
But now they have faded,
Those beauties in red,
And living is jaded
When true love is bled.

He sent me white roses,
Pale ghosts of the red,
Pure white-petalled roses
For happiness fled.[1]

#

His exercise is limited now to slowly walking around the block several times a day. Crossing streets that would introduce new sounds and the shadows of new structures, is too difficult. Even with his white cane he can't be sure that he'll be missed by the traffic that whizzes by, too dicey, so he takes the safer route. He walks without having to

* This chapter is endnoted. The notes can be found at the end of this chapter.

cross streets, around the block, his block, daily, until he tires. Once safely home he takes out his magnifying glass and his pen that writes tall, thick letters, and prints out the verses that have entered his imaginative mind while he's been on his walk.

#

Swirling iridescent clouds
of unborn poems
are about me,
almost reachable
but swift moving,
provocative yet coy,
refusing to show their faces distinctly
yet now and again reaching toward me,
seeming to whisper
teasingly, expectantly.
Take me! Claim me!

Listening to the faint tones
of many almost-voices,
seeing a jeweled brightness
of an almost-substance,
I set an allure
of such inciting phrases
which might untangle
just one breath
of beauty
and hold it firmly, gently,
until the promise
of something delightful
is captured,
made my own possession
and breathes and lives and grows
into a poem.[2]

#

The phone rang. It was the poet. "Carrie's at hospice," he spoke.

"She's endured enough pain," he said, "and can't take the dialysis any more."

"I'll be over," I said, and I left the office. When I arrived, he was waiting at his front door.

Carrie was a neighbor whose home was on the path which the poet took on his daily exercise. She was only 41 but following a car accident several years ago — her vehicle was rear-ended — her kidneys were affected, just stopped their efficient filtering of her body poisons. She was living by using a dialysis machine three times a week, five hours a day, portal to portal, four hours on the mechanical arachnid that sucked the blood from her body and then regurgitated it in purer form.

She was surrounded by misery, one of many patients in a large room at the D' Center. Everyone there showed the effects of illness, some without all their limbs, others near-crazed from the burden the treatment imposed; most exhausted, long-suffering, their strength tapped from their body's poisons, and all affected with the love-hate emotions felt towards the frightening, apathetic machines to which they feel always conjoined, life-saving for awhile, until they can stand them no longer. Carrie had reached that pinnacle. For her it was time. She would suffer them no more.

Carrie's body showed the effects of her debilitating treatment, the price of continued life. Her thighs protruding from summer shorts were thin as upper arms; the remnant of a once pretty face was a visage that no longer smiled. But she liked the poet, and he, her, and on his travels around the block Carrie would sometimes call out to him, or phone him first, before he left his nearby home, suggesting that he stop by, come in, rest and visit. Once there he would recite some of his verses to her. Together, they were entertained, considerate friends. Her renal illness and his minimal vision were not obstacles to their mutual kindness and affection. "Papa," she called him, like grandfather.

"She might live four or five days at hospice," he thought, until her body's venomous poisons consume her. And with hopeful countenance, a dominant wish not just an afterthought, he offered that "she might change her mind."

I just listened, nodding when appropriate although he may not have detected the motion. We stood at his front door. I wasn't invited in, so we both stood, talking, listening, on the porch stoop.

An hour passed. "I'd better let you go," the poet said. He was talked-out by then. He'd told me and repeated the same stories several times — important moments that he and Carrie shared in their friendship. He knew that he was repeating but the moments were important. He was reliving them, memories that would be sustaining, and which might be the substance of new verses to be rhymed in future days.

The second call from the poet came the following day, less than 24 hours since Carrie had laid her weakened body on the hospice bed. "On line two," the receptionist spoke — "the poet."

"Carrie just died!" This was an announcement that he expected to make, but not this soon, and these three words were difficult for him to voice. He had just lost one who was like a loving grandchild to him, someone who listened, who encouraged him, who provided the comfort of friendship.

"I'm not going to the funeral," he continued. "That would be too hard."

"Peering into the ominous blackness... pondering [this] darkness"[3] he wished not to do — not at least in formal setting with others who mourned her passing, too. He will mourn alone, and he is mourning now.

#

...Suddenly he pauses, listens intently;
[to] the sound of something in the dark outside,
Something there, is calling him . . . .
Something is out there,
Shivering or slinking in the blackness, and calling.
The stillness of the room begins to tense
as night sounds beyond the walls become noisily restless.
The wind and distant thunder
and the clicking sleet are speaking,
calling to him.
Slowly, wearily the old one drags himself
to the rattling door, [and] opens it.
'If [you're] out there,' he
tries to shout,
'the door [is] open.'[4]

#

Grief is revisited with the poet's loss of this special friend. She was one who listened, who cared, who broke the isolation of the summer days for him; who called to see that he was okay each dawn, except, of course, those three days every week when she was renewing her life on the D' machine. She encouraged his writing, his verse, the inscription of his feelings on paper so that these messages will be saved for others and savored by them, too. And the loss of her friendship, the death of someone who cared for him and gave his life expectancy is not quick in passing. Her calls have stopped. There is no one in her little house around the bend in his block. The blinds are drawn, the door is closed. The stoop is empty. And his own life is made vulnerable now; the ominous blackness about which his poetry speaks is more visible now, louder now — "...the sound of death in the dark outside."[5]

I went by the poet's home again that day, midafternoon. He was sleeping and the door noise — a rasping bell — caused him to suddenly awake. Without his hearing aids I was required to speak loudly. He never put them on during this visit and that caused him to talk loudly, too. That was all right. There was nothing I could say that he needed to hear. Shouting by him, loudly enough for him to hear himself was, I suspect, helpful. When loss occurs it's no time to be quiet. And I had been invited inside this time, removed from the hot summer air, and with the doors shut no one could be disturbed by our loud conversation. He misses Carrie and is grieving, and he can be as loud and as talkative as he wants to be.

An hour passes; he seems relieved, accepting of the unwanted reality. It will be difficult now for him to walk by the pretty, white clapboard home on his daily walks. He's strapped to a machine himself, the constant path around his block, the only route he can walk with safety because of the "dark outside" — caused by his blindness — the death of his sight. But he is ready, he says, to venture out. He knows his life is changed. But, hopeful still, there is tomorrow and it may bring a treasure not felt today.

#

They thought it strange,
Seeing the Old One smiling at the sunset
As though there were something he could see
That night could not destroy.

'There are two jewels,' he said,
'That warm the heart against all cold.
So long as you have them, keep them, [and]
Life cannot pass you by.'

Wherever there is Hope, there is life;
And so long as Expectancy
Empowers and fires the soul,
Just so long do you live.

'I am searching the sunset,' he said,
'For the promise of tomorrow.
It is then that I shall know
The meaning of today.'[6]

ENDNOTES TO CARRIE

1. "He Sent Me White Roses," Clifton B. Kruse, Sr., *Alone Together*, Tee-Town Printers, Topeka, Kansas (1997), p. 140.
2. "Inspiration," *id.*, p. 85.
3. "Exit," *id.*, p. 193.
4. *Id.*, p. 194. The poet ends the rather long verse by saying . . . "Life always goes on, even though we can never be sure just where it is going — or why, either." Death entered the poet's doorway on January 4, 2000.
5. *Exit*, *id.*
6. "Two Jewels," *id.*, p. 155.

*Disposable Humanity — Do Elders Have a Duty to Die?**[1]

The loss of biographical status,[2] the disappearance of importance as persons, is a reality in this country's community of frail[3] elders — the congregation[4] that we are dedicated to professionally serve.

Professor David Lyons, in his essays on law, justice, and political responsibility, collectively entitled, *Moral Aspects of Legal Theory*,[5] suggests that "[f]ar more often than not, law has served oppressive, unjust, [and] inhumane social arrangements.... [While law is not] ... inherently evil, [it serves] injustice as well as justice."[6] We define "justice" to mean the satisfaction of values that we personally admire, however idiosyncratic such values may appear when measured by populist ethics and politics.[7]

In defining the purpose of Law, Lyons observes that some writers posture "... that life without law would be nasty, brutish and short. The trouble [with that argument] is that life [is] like that for [many, older persons currently] living under [our country's] Law.[8]

Barbara J. Logue writes in her excellent text, *Last Rights — Death Control and the Elderly in America*,[9] that the nation's seven million chronically ill elders share the last rung when the country's needs are prioritized.[10] She writes, "When the United Nations asked governments to identify major issues of concern for mortality and morbidity policy, none of the eighty-three countries mentioned the aged.... Of twenty-nine Economic Commission for European Nations surveyed in recent years ... only Norway responded that the illnesses of the aged population [are] of special concern."[11] Such inattention suggests the conclusion that their humanity is presumed unimportant and as such, is disposable.

Laws that our country enacts which affect the elderly among us may be unjust, brutish[12] and socially destructive to them. The Omnibus Budget Reconciliation Act of 1993 (OBRA)[13] '93, for example, with its harsh insistence on estate recovery,[14] and repayment of public benefits received at the death of disabled trust[15] beneficiaries is illustrative unlike other benefits programs, such as Aid to Dependent Children (ADC), Supplemental Security Income (SSI), and Medicare, which do not extract repayment from the deceased recipients' estates or from their families.

The elders' values — the desire to be independent, to be cared for in their own homes, their place of familiar security, and their desire to leave something of theirs behind — an inheritance for those who follow them — social immortality for the donors,[16] are ruptured when elders are economically dependent, i.e., when they have

* This chapter is endnoted. The notes can be found at the end of this chapter.

insufficient funds for necessary long term care. These desires, not politically recognized as deserved, are secondary to national mores seen as more worthy. Frailty resulting in social and economic unproductivity make near moribund persons who are considered valueless, politically unimportant. Quality of life issues, including the recognition of the importance of responsibly satisfying such persons' reasonable end-life expectations, are unnoticed. While the government in passing recognition of humanity may design "... a plethora of [institutional] regulations [to] ensure that bedpans are counted and clocks are punched, no one [in government] seems to know how to measure quality of life, let alone produce it, for frail elders[,]" whose vitality as social persons has gone.[17]

We are not necessarily experiencing an abandonment of human values as a new phenomena. American towns in the colonial period "weaned out," denied settlement for persons anticipated as dependents and who had little to contribute. Frail older persons were perceived as unworthy of care.[18] "Excessive longevity (survival beyond one's ability to make positive contributions to family or society) is universally disvalued."[19] This impulse may be increased in prominence where a community feels the pressure of competing applications among those that must share the country's fisc,[20] as we now do in a country where some politicians are determined to reduce its current federal budget by one trillion dollars.[21]

Families, as well as communities, have limited endurance for decrepitude. Tolerance of frailty equates to the disabled elders' economic independence. Where the elders' wealth has not yet been consumed or relinquished or lost by appropriation, they are endured. Older persons, particularly those who are feeble, tend to be valued in direct proportion to what they can still do for younger generations, including their family members.[22] Prolonged dependency, irreversibly declining health, and the disappearance of their own sources of economic independence, recasts the importance of the dependent elder both to his or her family as well as to the communities in which such persons live.[23]

Our awareness of this animality feature of our humanity may cause us to be better lawyers, more insightful family counselors, more protective agents for our charges whose values and biographical importance should not end with fragility. Hastened death because elder care is not a national priority should not be quietly tolerated. Our fragile ancestral community, however unproductive they may be, has no duty to die.

ENDNOTES TO DISPOSABLE HUMANITY

1. A suggestion by Colorado's former governor, Richard Lamm, arguably misinterpreted by the popular press, implied that there is a moral duty to die when one reaches a certain degree of decrepitude.
2. Dementia patients particularly "... often are the defenseless targets of long-term care staff who, guided by the belief that loss of cognitive ability diminishes a person's humanity, dismiss residents with dementia as beyond help and unworthy of care." Jennifer Foote, "Dementia — Abuse and Neglect Compound the Suffering of Many Elderly," *Sunday Star-Ledger*, New Jersey (May 7, 1995), p. 1.
3. By frail is meant physically fragile and delicate; significantly demented, feeble and dependent. "Today nursing homes and other long term care facilities [where our frail elder clients may be housed] are defacto psychiatric wards.... [T]he facilities are failing in many cases to deliver even marginal care to elders with dementia.... [Patients] are taken care of the way we [cared for] psychiatric patients 150 years ago... [and] measures specifically designed [by the federal government] to improve the quality of care for dementia patients have largely failed." *Id.*
4. For purposes of this text, congregation is defined as the collection of elders in our various communities, not necessarily congregated together.
5. Cambridge Un. Press (1993).
6. *Id.* Preface, p. IX.
7. At least for purposes of this article, "justice" is defined in this way, perhaps fairer than the philosophers wry suggestion that "[m]ight is right and justice there is none." Walther von der Vogelweide (1170-1230), *Millennium*, (no publication date available). *Bartlett's Familiar Quotations, Little Brown & Co.* (1992). This statement in an apparent corrupted version reads, "might is right and justice is the stronger of the two."
8. *Id.* p. X. Lyons uses "most persons" rather than "many older persons." It does not appear to the author of this essay that this modification depreciates Lyons' broader assertion.
9. MacMillan (1993).
10. *Id.* pp. 56, 54.
11. *Id.* pp. 56, 55. In this country, "[t]ypically, it is the most vulnerable who are the first to suffer when cost considerations arise. The most explicit rationing efforts to date — those associated with Diagnosis Related Groups (DRGs) — are aimed at elderly Medicare patients. Enacted in 1983 under the Medicare program, the DRG prospective payment system was designed to contain costs by paying hospitals a fixed amount per patient, based on ... diagnosis and other factors. If a hospital keeps a patient an unnecessarily long time or performs unnecessary tests, it loses money.

Other incentives in the system encourage earlier discharge — 'quicker and sicker' — and so entail a risk of inadequate care. Alternatively, since payment is the same for simple and complicated cases in the same diagnostic category, hospitals may cut corners or even refuse admission to sicker patients, whose costs of care threaten to exceed the payment rate. Most important, both Medicare and Medicaid are increasingly reluctant to finance long-term care, and nursing homes select against heavy care cases that are more costly in terms of staff time as well as monies. For example, when Frank Robinson tried to find a suitable nursing home for his ailing mother, the social worker told him, 'Let's face it, nobody wants her. She's too heavy. They prefer the little skinny, eighty-pounders. And she can't go to the bathroom to relieve herself. She needs too much nursing.' Hence the lives of the frailest continue to be low priority, and little community fuss is made about it. [citations omitted]." *Id.* pp. 53-54.

12. By brutish is meant, at best, unpleasant and, at worst, violent.
13. Public Law No. 103—6 (H.R. 2264, S. 1134), Revenue Reconciliation Act of 1993, §§ 13611, 13612.
14. 42 U.S.C. § 1396p(b)(4).
15. 42 U.S.C. § 1396p(d)(4)(A) and (d)(4)(B) and (d)(4)(C).
16. Joel C. Dobris, "Divestment of Assets to Qualify for Medicaid...," *An Aging World — Dilemmas and Challenges for Law and Social Policy*, ed. by John Eekelaar and David Pearl, Clarendon Press, Oxford (1989), pp. 791-804.
17. *Supra* n.9, pp. 53, 32. Not in government, but to the contrary in nursing home administration. See Thomas, William H., M.D., *Life Worth Living (How Someone You Love Can Still Enjoy Life in a Nursing Home)*, VanderWyk & Burnham, Acton, Mass., (1997).
18. *Id.* p. 32.
19. *Id.* p. 30.
20. *Id.* p. 26. See also Peter Singer, *The Collapse of Our Traditional Ethics*, (N.Y., St. Martin's Press); the New York Times Book Review (May 7, 1995), p. 7.
21. David E. Rosenbaum, "Senate Approves Proposal to Balance Budget by 2002 ...." *The New York Times*, Fri., May 26, 1995.
22. *Id.* pp. 29, 24.
23. *Id.* pp. 22-25. "Popular opinion in preindustrial France held that 'old age was a horror and old people a great nuisance.'" Id. p. 29.

Three Trusts and a Will

"Well, good afternoon." I greeted two ladies in the reception room as they arrived from a small town 100 miles away. "Coffee?" I inquired — "It's Starbuck's®, the house special blend. Tea? Water?"

Nothing, it turned out. The two appeared no worse for wear following their long drive to the lawyer's office, and they wanted to get down to business. They had no interest in improvised Cachaca of any kind. They still faced a return trip when this meeting was over — unfortunately timed such that they'll hit the rush-hour traffic on their return.

One of the two was well-dressed, impressively coiffured, and carried a briefcase, a large, old style Samsonite®, made in Denver at a now-extinct manufacturing plant south of downtown. It looked well-used, and it was full. Large envelopes, stock records, a thick and worn checkbook — three checks to a page-size, pens, scissors and tape could be seen when the lid was opened. Its bearer was an investment advisor, and was accompanying her short, dowdy, client-companion; she was along to help.

The client was perhaps 5'2". At age 64 her short bangs-cut dutchboy hair arrangement exposed her neck fully. It bore no jewelry. Her hair, a light shade of brown, was graying. Dull and unfashionable, it also looked unwashed. I saw no cosmetic use. She wore a pale blue jacket with a front zipper, the kind one might wear to an evening baseball game, Woolworth-style one size fits all polyester slacks, and comfortable but not dressy shoes. Garden shoes, I'd call them. And they were not polished. An interesting pair, these two. They didn't match. Their relationship with each other I surmised, certainly, was not social.

"My daughter gave me your name, picked it out of Martindale-something," the short one said.

"Great," I responded. "Actually your daughter called me, checked me out, and asked if I could see you." Daughter was a lawyer, but she and her mother were separated by too many states. Daughter didn't see her mother often, and didn't have any contacts with lawyers here.

"I want a trust and a will." She paused, but wasn't finished, "and I want trusts for my daughters, too."

"Three trusts and a will?"

"Yes. How much?"

"What kind of trusts are they to be? What will the trusts provide? Why trusts for your daughters anyway, and why a trust for you? And what's to go in them — what will you be transferring? Hold on to your 'how much' question. I'll give you an estimate before you leave. Now why three trusts and a will?"

"I want to divide my assets three ways and put my daughters' shares in trust for them until they're 55."

"Why?" I asked.

"Because one daughter can't manage money, and you have to treat them the same."

"You do? How old are they?"

"Thirty-five and forty-one," their mother answered, daughters in mid-life, fully adult. The one who's forty-one is a lawyer, but doesn't make much money, and the one who is thirty-five is on her third husband, "looking for a fourth," mom said. I left that line alone.

Had I understood her correctly? She wants to create trusts for her daughters now, divide her estate three ways, two-thirds to them? I had. She confirmed it. This is what she intends doing. Her daughters' shares are to be held in complex, accumulation trusts. Reinvesting the income the funds will appreciate in value, distributing nothing to the respective beneficiaries until each daughter celebrates her 55th birthday. The trusts dissolve then and each daughter-beneficiary receives its bounty.

"Want to talk tax issues, tax detriments in the trusts you've described?"

"No," she said, "that's not my problem."

"It's not?"

"No." Well, I thought to myself, perhaps I can get back to this later.

"What do you own?"

The companion with the big brief case made her entry into the conversation, interjected, gave me a list of securities, $270,000.00 in value, $20,000.00 in cash. Her client owned a small home worth only $35,000.00 resting as it did, in a Colorado mountain town, near no chair lifts that attract the skiing community, the big spenders who own 4-wheel drive Range Rovers®, and carry plenty of cash. Old homesteads quickly accelerate the price of the level ground they're on, desired as getaways by the weekend crowd. But with no groomed snow slopes nearby such a windfall wouldn't apply here.

"Anything else?" I wondered aloud.

"$70,000.00," the short one added, "my furniture and stuff."

"Antiques?" I asked.

"It's all old."

"Over 100 years?"

"No."

"No antiques. What do you have that's worth $70,000.00?"

"Well, maybe $60,000.00."

"What would your neighbors pay you for your collection? What would it bring in the big city?"

She shrugged her shoulders.

"Less value, less tax," I teased.

"It's not worth much," she confessed. So much then for the tangibles.

"So you've got a little over $300,000.00, plus your furniture and household things."

"More like $400,000.00," the briefcase carrier said, "maybe $500,000.00."

"Okay, what did I miss? Stock — cash — house — any life insurance?"

"No."

"Retirement, like an IRA?"

"Just Social Security — $780.00 a month."

"Is $325,000.00 fair?" I looked directly into my client's eyes.

"Yeah, probably."

"Over a third of a million," I said, not wanting to demean the widow's small stash — not much divided three ways. But there had to be a reason for this lady's sudden need to gift most of her wealth to her two daughters — daughters she couldn't trust to use their shares wisely — at least at this point in time. I wondered what was really going on. Why make gifts now? Why put the assets in trusts? Why go through filing gift tax returns? Why give away assets that have surely grown in value that will assure payment of tax on the capital gain when the appreciated assets are sold?

I raised these questions. She had no answers. She just wanted the trusts drawn. But I couldn't in good conscience prepare these documents. They wouldn't be revocable, and with her daughters' shares she couldn't change her mind. I needed to find out why she felt impelled to do this. She needed to be able to tell me. She couldn't, or wouldn't at least not yet. I had to start poking around elsewhere to get the answer to why.

"How's your health?" I asked.

This question was followed by a long pause.... She began to cry. Another half minute passed. I waited her out.

"It's not good."

I didn't respond. "Sugar diabetes, high blood pressure..." she offered after a few moments. I was sure, however, that I was not getting the full list.

"Any illnesses that are terminal?" I asked, a question that's not routine.

"No," she replied quickly, too quickly, and she wasn't looking at me. I was prying, asking about things she felt I didn't need to know. Her gaze was now on the tabletop in front of her.

"I don't want them to get it until they're 55."

"A trust created by your will can provide for that, and then, all of your assets will be fully available to you as long as you live."

More tears.

I always try to wait them out; let the tears flow. This client needed the tension released that this tearful cleansing may bring. Her companion, however, was on to business, offered comments to our mutual client ignoring her discomfort, intending to be helpful: "I'm not a lawyer, but what about a Crummey Trust?" she asked, "or annual gifts into trusts for your daughters?" were two such insipid offerings.

The interview was going nowhere and I could sense my client's frustration. In her mind, what she wanted was simple — three trusts and a will. Presumably her one-third would be comprised primarily of the house and furniture, her daughters' two-thirds would be made up of the investments, taken, of course, at mom's cost basis assuring capital gain taxes later. That she would have no investments left once such trusts are funded mattered not to her — perhaps, I feared, because of an intended foreshortened life.

My client's nonsybaritic dress, her vimless demeanor, the flat affect in her voice, her disinterest in discussing the consequences of the plans she had devised, sounded to me like she's giving up, preparing for death, perhaps planning it.

"Are you depressed?" I softly asked. She looked away.... "Tell him," said the investment counselor, but my client said nothing.

"She's been hospitalized for depression," her investment advisor snitched.

"On medications?" I gently asked, looking at my client, but there was no response.

An hour had passed, a tough sixty minutes for this lady who will have traveled 200 miles today to instruct a lawyer to draft three trusts and a will. She stood up. She'd had enough. We got too close, too fast, with company in the room, someone she had trusted, but who had snitched.

"How much do I owe you?" she asked.

"You don't owe me anything," I replied. "And, I'm sorry that I can't draw the documents for you that you say you need; just like your doctor, a surgeon can't operate without knowing why."

We stamped their parking receipt and the couple left my private office prepared to head back, the dowdy one to what I suspect is not much more than a shack in the Rockies. It will be a long drive home for them.

Hospitalized for depression, could this mean the State Hospital, the asylum for the mentally ill? Is this plain and simple and unhappy lady planning to foreshorten her life, setting up trusts for her mid-life adolescent daughters, protecting two-thirds of their inheritance until they are on the down side of middle age? Is she arranging her release from any further responsibility to her remaining family, still seen as dependent and immature, so that she can end her depression by her own hand because hospitalization hasn't worked?

There was no reasonable opportunity to discover the answers to these questions. I would like to know who her doctor is and if she will let me speak to her or him; what medications she is taking, and whether or not she is fantasizing about her own death.

Exposed by her friend — "She's been hospitalized for depression" — her anguish is secret no longer. Premature, not yet comfortable enough to talk about this episode with a stranger — a lawyer whose name was handy, picked out of a book, over a few hills and dales, but nonetheless reachable, was too stressful. He asked questions that she couldn't comfortably answer, and wouldn't do as she had instructed, wouldn't draft three trusts and a will for her.

"You're welcome to come back," I offered as the two were leaving. They were at the elevator entry, and the doors opened to take this odd couple back to the parking level below. "I want three trusts and a will," was the frumpish one's simple request. What could be so hard about doing that? She didn't know, couldn't understand. My client's eyes, squinty now, stared away, beyond me, her mind bewildered. Unable to help, I watched our final parting as the closing doors enveloped them.

"Because I Like It Here"*

A frail elder, in his late 80s, dying of kidney disease and cancer, was recently disengaged from life-support technology. His living will required this following 48 hours after he was diagnosed as terminally ill, provided that he was also in an unconscious state. These preconditions had been satisfied.

Regaining consciousness following removal of life-support, and after leaving the hospital and returning to his bed at his group home, he responded to the question, "Do you still want your living will enforced if a similar crisis occurs?" with an unmistakable and emphatic, "No!" "Why?" his lawyer asked. "Because," he responded, "I like it here."[1]

Limited as he was, to a bedridden state, with one useless kidney and one cancerous companion, that dutifully tried, but at best inadequately to remove his nitrogenous wastes, a significantly restricted life was better, he felt, than none at all. He lived courageously and continued to find entertainment in his limited habitation. But he had executed a living will when he was younger, more healthy, and vertical in posture. He could not at that earlier time imagine wanting to live a life of significantly lesser joy.

#

When Hippocrates was born, about 460 B.C.E.,[2] illness was believed caused by supernatural forces. Ancient theurgy held that divine agency was necessary in the cure of disease.[3] Hippocrates, well known for the physician's oath,[4] introduced a medical theory about illness that was founded upon empiricism.[5] He believed that cure for disease was both natural and discoverable, determined by cause and effect, and had nothing to do with the supernatural nor with magic.[6]

Notwithstanding this beginning and the prescient insight of this early physician, it wasn't until the Sixteenth Century, about two thousand years after Hippocrates's death, that knowledge about the internal anatomical structures of human beings was known.[7] William Harvey, proved by demonstration in the year 1616, that the human heart did not contain "innate heat,"[8] but was a mechanical device that pumped blood through the body in a continuous circuit. Not until that time did our medical pioneers understand the function of the heart, what is now unquestioned and comprehensible to us.[9]

More than two millennia have passed since empirical medicine was first recognized. Important medical innovations have followed including improvement in the diagnosis of illness, the realization that unseen germs cause sickness and death, the discovery that cells are the basic units where disease begins, the compounding of helpful medicines

* This chapter is extensively endnoted because of the subject matter, the medical advance-directive, the living will. The notes can be found at the end of this chapter.

and anodynes, surgery without pain, and organ transplantation, for example, but by 1900 there still remained few effective treatments for life-threatening diseases.[10]

Surgeons still operated in frock coats stiff with blood and filth in the last century, and asepsis, disinfecting the operating area, and antisepsis, sterilizing the wound area itself, was not common until 100 years ago.[11]

Major advances in life-sustaining technology did not begin until the 1920s, only 75 years ago. Insulin was discovered in 1921, making treatment for diabetes possible. Ten years later the first mechanical ventilator, the "iron lung," was invented and sulfa drugs and penicillin, preventing the growth of disease-causing bacteria, were discovered and synthesized.

The artificial kidney was crafted during the 1940s, its appearance stimulated by injuries to U.S. military forces in World War II. In the 1950s, open-heart surgery, coupled with the discovery of polio vaccine, the improvement of mechanical ventilators, and the first use of intensive care units (ICUs) were that decade's medical innovations.

Cardiopulmonary resuscitation (CPR) did not exist until the 1960s, and in those years, "...coronary artery bypass surgery, kidney transplants, total parenteral nutrition...radio-therapy[12] and chemotherapy...were introduced. Coronary care units (CCUs) were established [at this time as well]..."[13] The 1960s witnessed the first transplanted heart.[14]

The decade of the '70s continued major advances in life-sustaining medical breakthroughs "...in the treatment of cancer, heart disease, heart attack and stroke." [15] In 1979, cyclosporine was introduced, making it possible to reduce immunological rejection in the transplantation of tissues.[16] In the 1980s,[17] "...an artificial heart was placed in a living patient for the first time.[18]

Exponentially, new technologies affecting life-threatening disease and illnesses are predicted.[19] In the '90s, we have discovered that genes on chromosomes 1 and 14 may account for familial Alzheimer's Disease,[20] for example, and the development of technologies in the next five to fifteen years are predicted that will positively affect human life by improvements in the areas "...of artificial and transplanted organs and tissues; cancer vaccines; implantable drug delivery systems for cancer and other diseases and [the creation of] immunosuppressive drugs."[21]

Rapidly developing abilities of the medical community in this country to prolong life in cases where, historically, the illness or disease would otherwise be fatal, is reasonably expected in this century.

In this medical environment, is the "Living Will," the initial incursion into medical autonomy, the document relied on by the one who discovered in his frailty that he still "liked it here," antiquated? Is such a directive now unreasonably used by our clients? The living will presumes a disposition that its signers, whether near-moribund or significantly fragile, will not want to continue living with life-support strategies, even though such procedures may not be invasive.[22]

When one makes a decision to execute a Living Will, such person is generally both vertical in posture and healthy, what our ancestors would call being in good humor.23 When the Living Will is acted upon, its signer is horizontal, "in bad humor," and diseased, even though still alive. Do we consider life differently when we are in that posture and condition, and is the natural longing to live such that, withholding technologies for life support, is contrary to what some human beings at that point in their lives will want?[24]

By their intrinsic nature, living wills are poorly considered and are not reasonably followed as protocols for health care providers, applied as they are, at a time when the patient may no longer rationally participate in medical decision making.[25] There may be asymmetry in the values that one expresses when in relatively good health, and the values that replace those opinions when one's life is on the line and where new and innovative treatment may, in fact, not be futile.[26] As we age, we accommodate to lesser abilities, reduced energy, poorer memories, and with other frailties that are part of this process. Even as our health is compromised, our quality of life reduced, our disorders permanent, our prognosis discouraging, we accommodate, and perhaps much to our surprise, even with our infirmities, continue to enjoy life. We still like it here.

This message suggests caution in using directives that conclude in advance of disease and illness, and absent futility, that some in the assemblage of ill will want what the medical community may be able to provide them at that later point in time.

The legal and educational program director for Choice In Dying, has suggested that "Living Wills empower patients by making sure [that] their wishes are obeyed."[27] This assumes, however, a psychology of the declarant that is unchanged, and particularly with foreseeable medical advances on the horizon, that just may not be so.[28]

ENDNOTES TO BECAUSE I LIKE IT HERE

1. This is one of several incidents in the author's practice which suggests that caution be exercised in recommending that living wills be executed. Available in all states but subject to legislative variation, in Colorado *see* Colorado Medical Treatment Decision Act, 15-18-101, et seq., Colorado Revised Statutes.
2. B.C.E.: Before the Common Era. Hippocrates's birth was on the Western Coast of Asia Minor. His writings deal with a study of duty, deontological concepts. Certain behavior is necessary because it is the right thing to do, a moral obligation. *See Sherwin B. Nuland, Doctors: The Biography of Medicine*, (Random House, Inc., N.Y., 1988, Second Vintage Books Edition, January, 1995), p. 24.
3. Theurgy, a magical science of the neoplatonists, involved the use of magical acts in securing intervention. Neoplatonism was dominant from the Third to the Sixth Centuries, A.D., based on the work of Plato and developed by Plotinus.
4. The oath is set out in *Nuland*, supra n. 2, p. 26. The ethical code " . . . was a proof to patients . . . that [the] doctor . . . typified a different order of healer than did the imposters who roamed the land in pursuit of the purses of the sick," p. 23.
5. The " . . . injunction to turn a blind eye to the possibility of a deity or mystical influence in the causes and treatment of disease was the greatest contribution made by . . . Hippocrates." Id., p. 4.
6. *Id.*, p. 4, 7. Neoplatonists attributed cure to magical science, theurgy to divine intervention. Neoplatonism was a philosophical and religious system that combined both Platonic thought and Oriental mysticism. *See The Concise Oxford Dictionary* (8th Ed., 1990), p. 796.
7. Historically, there has been a basic horror of corpses, and proscriptions against human dissection. *Supra* n. 2, p. 9. The Catholic Church would not allow dissections until the Thirteenth Century. *Id.*, p. 153. Thereafter, " . . . the forces of the dissectors and the chemists who sought answers in organs, then in tissues, and finally, [and only relatively recently] within the structure of the cell itself." *Id.*, p. 10. Morgaani, credited with being the father of pathological anatomy, is the founder of modern medical diagnosis. *Id.*, p. xvii and p. 161. He graduated from medical school at age 19 in 1701. *Id.*, p. 175.
8. In Hippocrates's age, and prior to the Fifth Century, the heart was thought to contain "innate heat," a form of energy generated by the heart, Id., p. 13, and " . . . disease was thought . . . to be caused by an imbalance among [four body effluvia, anciently called], 'humors' — blood, yellow bile, black bile, and phlegm. These four primary fluids were said to be constantly renewed by means of the food which is eaten and digested. The blood was thought to originate in the heart, the yellow bile in the liver, the black bile in the spleen, and the phlegm in the brain." *Id.*

Observe that our language and literature remains affected by this theory of disease and illness over two and one-half later. We hear a description of someone said to be (or not to be) in "good humor." Dispositions are described as sanguine, optimistic, confident (blood); melancholic (defined as a black bile humor in Oxford, supra, n. 5, p. 739; bilious, bad tempered (Latin *bilosus*, f. *billis*); or phlegmatic (sluggishness attributed to too much phlegm in the constitution), *See Oxford*, *supra* n. 5, p. 894. *Doctors, supra* n. 2, pp. 14, 48, 134.

9. *Doctors*, *Id.*, pp. 134-135.
10. *Life-Sustaining Technologies and the Elderly*, U.S. Congress, Office of Technology Assessment (OTA-BA-36, Wash., D.C., U.S. Gov't. Printing Office, July 1987, Lib. Congress #87-619835), p. 39.
11. Joseph Lister established the modern aseptic ritual in 1891. *Supra*, n. 2, p. 382.
12. The treatment of disease by X-rays or other forms of radiation is referred to in this way. Molière's comedies include picturing the physicians of his day dressing in black robes and pointed hats and speaking in Latin. Surgery was performed by typically itinerant barber-physicians " . . . who were expert in sharp instruments if nothing else." Jacques Barzun, "The Professions Under Siege," *Harper's Magazine*, (October 1978), p. 61. *E.g.*, *see also*, Mozart, "The Marriage of Figaro," (1786).
13. *Id.*, p. 40.
14. *Id.* This occurred in 1967.
15. *Supra* n. 10, p. 40.
16. "The first liver transplant occurred in the 1970s, and heart and kidney transplants became more common. In 1985, about 600 people received liver transplants; 700 received heart transplants; and about 8,000 received kidney transplants." *Id.*, p. 40.
17. 1982.
18. *Id.*, p. 40.
19. *Id.*, p. 41.
20. *Science*, Vol. 269, (Aug. 8, 1995), p. 917; *See* "Physiologia," President's Report, *NAELA Quarterly*, Vol. 8, No. 4, (Fall 1995), p. 3, n. 6, reproduced in Part X of this book.
21. *Id.*, p. 41. *See also*, Nicholas Wade, "New Light Shed on How Enzymes May Play a Crucial Role in Cancer," *The New York Times*, (Sept. 5, 1995), p. B7. Citing the Sept. 1995 issue of the journal, *Science*, *Id.*, cancer cells have been found to evade cell death by activating the enzyme telomerase. Cells otherwise have a finite life, dying after dividing 70 times or so.
22. *Supra*, n. 10, p. 4. Selected life-sustaining technologies include drugs, medical devices, and procedures that can maintain an individual's life, who would otherwise die within a foreseeable, but usually uncertain time period. Five common tech-

nologies are: cardiopulmonary resuscitation (CPR), mechanical ventilation, renal dialysis, antibiotics, and nutritional support and hydration. Discussed pp. 4-5.

23. *See supra* n. 9.

24. In the thirty—day period following the death of Jacqueline Onassis, 11,000 persons called Choice In Dying about living wills. The usual number of monthly calls inquiring about this subject is 2,200. The New York organization told *USA Today*, "Revived Interest in Living Wills," by Esme M. Infante, (Monday, May 23, 1994, p. 5D), that "we are seeing a much younger [and presumably healthier] population calling us — more men, more middle—aged [people] . . . . A lot of people figure 'someday I'll fill it out.' It takes [an Onassis] to drive it home that they should do it now and not wait."

25. Special Report, "Institutional Protocols for Decisions About Life-Sustaining Treatments," U.S. Congress, Office of Technology Assessment, (OTA-BA 389, Wash. D.C., U.S. Gov't. Printing Office, July 1988), p. 6.

26. *Gilgunn v. Mass. Gen. Hosp., Suffolk Sup. Ct., Commonwealth of Mass.*, No. 92—4820—H, 1995. The American Medical Association, in its Code of Ethics, provides that physicians are not ethically obligated to deliver care that, in their best professional judgment, will not have a reasonable chance of benefitting their patients. [Patients] are not entitled [to] treatments simply because they demand them. *See* Nat Hentoff, syndicated columnist, "When Physicians Ignore Their Patients Own Will to Live," *Gazette Telegraph*, Colorado Springs, Colo., 9-4-95, p. B-7. In the *Guilgunn* case, a 71-year-old patient suffered from heart disease, diabetes, chronic urinary tract infections, Parkinson's Disease, breast cancer (for which a mastectomy had been done), and experienced repeated seizures that resulted in brain damage and coma. The attending physician, supported by the hospital's Optimum Care committee, ordered a "do not resuscitate" order over the patient's daughter's objection, who advised medical staff that her mother had told her that "She wanted everything possible done medically." *Guilgunn* has been appealed.

27. Ann Fade, Choice in Dying, supra, n. 24.

28. The safer approach to advance directives generally is the Durable Agency Authorizing Medical Care, now available in most states. In Colorado, *See* Proxy Decision-makers for Medical Treatment, 15-18.5-101, et seq., C.R.S.

Postscript

If lawyers listen to their clients closely, they will describe their imagined intentions concerning death and dying. They speak almost to a person, bravely. "I don't want to be kept alive on a machine. Pull the plug. No heroics for me!" The conversation is frequently in the lawyer's office or at the client's home. Seldom is the subject discussed at the bedside of a hospitalized patient or in a nursing home unit, where the client now resides.

"What's plugged in?" the lawyer asks.

"Huh?" is the response.

"The machine — what machine that's keeping you alive do you want unplugged?"

Most of us are unaware that much life support is not invasive; we can be in the hospital quite ill, and nothing attached to our body will be plugged in. And if we are gasping for breath, requiring oxygen to be forced into our lungs — needing a machine that breathes for us, is it not to be employed?

My experience standing by clients' bedsides, called in by their families to come to the hospital because their loved one is not doing well, is that the "living will" issue will be brought up. The family wants to know what to do. Where the patient is conscious and is reminded by us that a living will has been signed (an instruction not to continue life support if one is terminally ill), there is most often a change of heart. Terminal illness, a death predicted within a short time period, typically six months,

still means that the grim reaper is not yet present in the room. If a terminally ill patient is unconscious or "otherwise incompetent" (Colorado's statutory Living Will language), then the "plug is to be pulled" and may not now be a palatable direction. Decisions made in horizontal positions — when the patient now faces the reality of death — are frequently contrary to the decision voiced with bravado by the patient when he or she was vertical, upright and feeling well. That's what this last essay, "Because I Like it Here," is about.

Where pain is controlled and depression is mild, death is considered but not invited by many elders. They may toy with the thought of suicide and may even want to discuss it, but for a Kevorkian response, (terminate my life, please), more severe depression and significant pain must surely be a threshold. Where there are still positive memories, and despair has not yet become a constant visitor, the option by the ill patient is not infrequently for continuation of life. "Because I Like It Here" reminds us of this reality.

"Carrie," (Chapter 12), on the other hand, was visited by constant hopelessness. She was in anguish and surely depressed, revived periodically by the poet's visits, her vision of life lived with no expectation of change, of wellness, of joy, and with no consciousness of how even minimal happiness might be achieved, she sought death, accepted it, and invited it to terminate her tragic and fragile life.

#

Lawyers who work with elders are aware that death may sometimes be planned. "Three Trusts and a Will," (Chapter 14), illustrates this. Such cases, seen as tragedies, alert elder lawyers to be even more insightful the next time. The patient's lawyer stands near the end of the line of would—be rescuers. Cues have been given to others, never effectively. Physicians stand in the front lines with family but don't always hear that which none of us want verbalized. And the clues given by patient-clients are unannounced and are often unheard.

"Disposable Humanity" is an essay first published in the *NAELA News*, a report to elder lawyers (members of NAELA, the National Academy of Elder Law Attorneys), who receive this publication. The essay announces that lawyers must be defenders of those clients they serve and that the attorney's role includes learning to be insightful counselors because the lawyer-counselor may be the last hope, the person to whom the final cue requesting help is given.

PART FIVE

*Human Encounters**

In June 1973, nine years following my graduation from law school, I sent a check for more than $50.00 to the Foundation Press in exchange for a book written by the prescient Dean of the Notre Dame Law School. Its title, *The Planning and Drafting of Wills and Trusts*,* understates its message. It is a book about human encounters — about the lawyer and the lawyer's client in congruent conversation.

Ruminating on the lawyers' in-school scholastic experience, the Dean observes that we are badly trained for the human encounters that we experience with our clients. Actually, the dean wrote, that we are poorly trained for the counseling opportunities that we will have with our clients in our law offices. But as lawyers who work with the elder community, our "offices" are often hospital rooms, nursing homes and the clients' own residences. As often as not, our contacts with our clients are in places other than the comfort of our own suites.

While the dean's text isolated its interest in lawyers preparing their clients' wills and trusts, our lack of adequate law school training applies to our work in helping older clients on a broader spectrum as well.

Our practices, as attorneys who work with elder clients (and sometimes with their families) are typically distanced from the competitive and litigious posture that is the fundament of our law school training. Ours is a relationship in which, as lawyers, we discern from our meetings with our clients much about their values and goals. We observe and listen and learn from them, participating in the discovery of solutions to the problems that are now disturbing their lives:

Why must I leave my home?

* Thomas L. Shaffer, *The Planning and Drafting of Wills and Trusts*, Foundation Press, Inc. (Mineola, NY 1972) This essay was written for elder lawyers and first appeared in the NAELA News. The pronouns "we" and "us" reflect this initial audience.

My doctors want to amputate my gangrenous toe. Don't let them take my foot. Please don't let them cut off my leg!

These portentous cries of anguish are not primarily questions of law, but not atypically, are problems reflecting an urgent desperation that the unfamilied elderly in particular ask us to resolve.

In law school we learned about rights and duties. This was our principal focus. The case book presentation evidenced persons in conflict, adversarial in posture, litigious in character and often rude in manner. In our intimate encounters with our clients, the *milieu* is one where needs and emotions are central, where decisions are premised on disturbingly critical issues of the moment for them.

As counselors in the elder law practice, we are wisely not orally aggressive; and we may not even be verbally sophisticated, common prerequisites of our colleagues who are members of the litigation bar. But our strength comes from accepting and caring for those who trust us as sensitive and educated friends. As elder law attorneys, lawyers dedicated to assisting clients with the legal and real life problems that age introduces to them, we develop a capacity to avoid quick answers — or any answers at all. Our responses are directed at assuring our clients that their solutions to the disruption of their lives that advanced age is causing are appropriate and wise — unless they are not. We achieve this by an openness, by a receptiveness to answers to our questions as we listen to those whose care has been entrusted to us — persons who often believe that their lives are over, clients who express their angst to us as we confront their grief and depression and anxiety. It is our routine experience in our work with near feckless older people.

We would have been married 69 years this November. I still remember meeting her.

And we say — "Tell me about her."

Her friends set it up.

"Set it up?" we reply.

Ninety minutes later, after telling and retelling his memory of the precious hours of the initial meeting that lead to a marriage of 60 years plus almost nine, the grief, at least for the moment, is lessened.

But clients are hesitant to share without invitation. There is a threshold that we must assure them that we want them to cross. And we do this with questions. And we do it as lawyers. We are the elders' lifeline. Medicaid planning, housing, wills, powers of attorney and trusts are the hardware that makes possible an invitation into the psyche of another, where a depressed spirit is enabled to share its load. Our licenses make this possible. They give us status and credibility, and after meeting us — hopefully, trust. The legal answers are comparatively easy — the job we are called in to do is done — but along the way, the more important, the more valuable service occurs as well. We listen. We invite a monologue. We establish this by our demeanor and by our questions that invite unloading — and in this process we extend the joy that elders' memories bring. And on those days, we earn the accolade — professional — one who serves others. That is our privileged role as lawyers; we can make others' lives, if even for a few moments, better than they were before.

We shouldn't be overly critical of the law schools and their curricula. They are better now than when some of us were graduated. There are elder law courses in some law schools now and counseling classes in some schools as well as practicums, opportunities to work with people and develop critical counseling skills. Such courses offset the utilitarian but less human centered values, for example, found in classes concerned primarily with such topics as mortgages, real property and taxes.

This is what the Notre Dame Dean tells us in his thin and costly book on drafting wills. He assures us that we are, as lawyers, at our best as counselors. It takes special people to work in the presence of emotion and grief and depression and with those for whom the "fun life" has essentially ended. Those among us who work in this area are our profession's heroines and heros. Our communities are blessed because of them, these lawyers who ennoble our profession.

"She Lived There, Too"

The chairs were arranged in a large circle — no head table. Whoever spoke at this meeting would be on center stage.

A group of fifteen, a community board for the city's Commission on Aging, had been recently formed and this was meeting three. One of its members, a highly respected specialist in international affairs, slumped down a bit in an uncomfortable chair, spoke out as the meeting began. He had said little, if anything at all, in meetings one and two, and at those initial gatherings when all chairs faced forward, had seated himself in a pew near the door.

"I'd like to know why I'm on this committee," he said. "Is it because I'm old?"

He is the eldest member of this group and he could be right. He may have been selected because of his age; that, indeed, could be the reason. This committee certainly has no interest in U.S. foreign policy.

"No, that's not the reason," the chair of the committee quickly asserted — the one who had, in fact, selected the group's members. "You have much to offer." But she didn't say what this was, and her response was followed by a rather long pause. The group was now all looking at him. It was his turn to speak again, and he changed the subject. "I have to leave early," he said, not raising himself from his slouch. "I'm being taken to Liberty Manor to see it today."

Liberty is an assisted living home north of the city, and as an adjunct, it contains a full-service nursing home wing. This member, the one inquiring about why he is here, is an alert, insightful 80-year old professor who still teaches a college class in foreign relations, and whose latest text on the subject, was, as he spoke, being delivered to book stores across the country. He is clearly not comfortable with an obligation that this day brings. For whatever reason "being taken . . . " sounds like this decision is not his, and "Liberty," the manor's name, is euphemistic, the antithesis of what he knows it to be.

"Being taken," were his words, not "I'm going to see," or "I'm checking out the manor — for housing and care later if I need it." This sudden blip in his schedule certainly didn't appear to be his idea.

The professor's contemplation is not invaded by his concerned listeners. He has more to say and this is a sensitive group. They wait for him to continue.

"But I want ("vant" was his pronunciation) to live in my home. I feel that I'm with my wife [there]." Several moments passed: his wife is deceased and his introspection is respected. He quietly continued, "She lived there, too."

Shared with us was his sad quondam, caring memories he wishes not to contuse.

I was curious why the professor's visit to the manor was scheduled to coincide with the gerontology meeting. Is he looking for allies, for ammunition that could be useful in replies he might be required to make in defense of his freedom — in rejecting Liberty Manor where someone, unnamed, is taking him on this morning, someone he's to meet for this purpose just moments from now?

He arose and walked sturdily across the room — no cane, no walker, no caregiver's arm needed. Mentally alert, physically able, the professor headed for the exit, and the committee began its scheduled agenda.

"Don't go!" I'd actually penned a note on a 3 x 5 card kept in my shirt pocket, but he was across the room and such a command required explanation, discussion, but "I'm being taken," was, in my mind, a clear cry for help, a suggestion of entrapment. He was up, leaving. Should I follow him out? I don't even know his name.

Perhaps "being taken" is a thoughtful phrase — someone is being kind, driving him to see the quod. He may have to live there someday, perhaps, so he's checking it out, albeit unenthusiastically, and then he'll return to his home. I quickly scanned the last meeting's minutes to see if his name was listed; no such luck, just committee business, no individual credits. He's not my client. I'm a stranger to him, and he to me. If I get up, follow him out, wouldn't I be interfering?

Suddenly he was gone, evaporated, but my inquietude didn't abate. A transition, I reason, that's what he's facing, stoically, perhaps even positively, but in leaving his home, if that happens now while he is alert and physically strong, there'll be more than just furnishings that will be irreparably left behind. I visualized the professor's home — his library, the place he writes his books, now perhaps with his wife gone, his desk replaced by the more convenient kitchen table, the markings in and about the house that he has made and that she made, too. He knows his home's nooks and crannies, his private hideaways and hers in a shared life there with his wife, whose presence he still feels. "I feel like I'm with my wife [when I'm in our home] .... She lived there, too." And her close presence remains felt by him in their place of memories; and he must talk to her there, say goodnight to her in her boudoir they surely shared, and he must affirm as dusk passes, ending each day, that he will see her in the morning, and following this nightly ritual, he restfully sleeps because he senses her presence there and she is watching over him and her, in their home where they may be alone together. Death has only denied their physical caresses, and when he arises he must feel her presence and must surely welcome her to the day that his continuing love for her enables him to perceive.

#

He is now gone and the phatic chatter of those attending the meeting is now occurring — words I couldn't hear, voices from bodies I didn't see, my attention consumed by thinking only of this one life, this 80-year-old stranger, who, despite his reputation, no one present really knew, invited to this meeting, he assumes, because he is old and not otherwise credentialed. He knows no one here, nor they him.

Will he return, I wonder? Does he feel abandoned by the faux-circle, one not included, not aided by helpful response to his woeful notice of capture, or ambush. "I'm being taken... and I don't vant to go." Can you hear me, feel with me what I feel — perhaps his call to us for help.

I imagined what his home was like — crumbs in the kitchen sink now used as his dining room table, piles of books and papers in his study, an unused and untouched living room, her clothes still in all but one of the home's closets, photographs of her displayed prominently on walls along the path he takes through the cluttered rooms of his home — their home.

Perhaps it's a well-meaning child who is taking him to Liberty. Maybe he has a son or daughter, picking him up to inspect what will surely be his last home in anticipation of his one day needing the care that will be available there. I'll come early to the circle's next rendevous, I resolve, introduce myself to him this time, ask how the visit went and listen.

#

Is this what the practice of elder law is about I wondered? Is it intervention, preventing insensitive others, including quisling children from serving a personal agenda? I visualized his child's daytimer organizer: *Friday*, take Dad to see the care center. *Saturday:* List the homestead for sale. Ignore its memories; discard all rubbish, advertise an estate sale, get rid of all the clutter. *Monday* (or as soon as the place sells): deposit the proceeds from the sale in a joint account, easier to get to when Dad leaves his asylum and joins Mother. *Tuesday:* talk to Dad about gifting, making it easier and less expensive for me when he dies: *Wednesday:* don't mention "Mom" to him; it's upsetting. He'll have companionship at Liberty, lots of ladies there. He'll be okay.

#

He didn't return — a no-show at the next meeting. No call to say that he would be absent. He didn't come to the meeting that followed either — a month later — no calls returned. His exit was permanent. We'd let him down — didn't intervene, but no one wanted to talk about it. The committee's agenda is too full. No time for quodlibet; no time for caring.

Postscript

"My kid oughta be a lawyer," not an uncommon comment by our clients whose child is in middle school, "because he likes to argue." The parents either watch too much t.v. or have witnessed trial lawyers in action, those whose demeanor is intense and combative. Many lawyers, actually most, however, argue very little. This is certainly true of those counselors in our communities whose practices include addressing the legal needs and concerns of the elder population, those in retirement, ill, confined to their homes, assisted living centers or nursing facilities. Here the attention is on winding up business affairs and planning for the transmission of wealth to the generations following. This group of individuals in our communities, now aged, is considering simpler housing, smaller places requiring less care, perhaps moving near their children. They're concerned with health, the specter of long term institutional care, whether Medicare will be lost, how to qualify for Medicaid in anticipation of the inability to financially care for themselves. They confront their own mortality; they're often alone and they are frightened.

When they get lucky, the lawyer they call is one who understands what elder law is about, and who knows it's first rule — listen to your client — use your third ear, the one that hears what the client is really saying — not just the words being used. That lawyer can identify the issues needing resolution — health care matters (Medicare and Medicaid); housing (assisting living centers, congregate homes, companions); wealth transmission (using wills and trusts); durable agencies (powers of attorney that transfer medical and financial decision-making to trusted family members or long-term friends), among a myriad of other elder law topics.

That's what "Human Encounters" is about, illustrated in "She Lived There, Too," essays written for aspiring elder-lawyers, as well as old-hands whose practices have included caring for the right side of the continuum of an aging population. The essays are reminders of what the elder lawyer must be — compassionate counselors at law, not mechanics, not persons who argue well, but problem solvers, counselors in the communities in which the elder lawyers practice making the lives of those residing in these villages and cities in our country better.

If you have a child who likes to listen, who cares about people, who wants to make a difference in the lives of others, those now distinguished by age — that's the child who "oughta be a lawyer."

PART SIX

"Take Peggy Out of My Will"

"Take Peggy out of my will!"

"Peggy?"

"You know — my eldest daughter."

That's how the conversation began with my first appointment of the day, a 79-year-old widow of 18 years. She has two children; Peggy is the older daughter, now 57; her sister is Carol.

Carol, now 54, is married and has one child, an 18-year-old son — and Carol has cancer. It has metastasized and now affects her lungs. She is receiving chemotherapy, and while the chemicals are keeping her alive for the moment, her mother volunteered that the cancer, she believes, is terminal.

What has Peggy done I wondered? Why disinheritance? This is going to be a tough visit. My client in late life is losing two daughters — one voluntarily.

"Tell me about Peggy," I asked. "Why this Will change?"

"She's abandoned the family, her sister — me! She has nothing to do with us, no calls, letters. She's angry with Carol. And she's told me that she's having no more to do with us."

#

It was a special weekend. My client is widowed and her two children arranged a mutual visit to see their mom over a holiday. They left their husbands at home. Peggy has no children; Carol's son, her only child, accompanied his mother. A niece was also visiting. It was a reunion taking place over a special holiday.

My client left the house for awhile. Her brief errand (on the second day of her daughters' planned three-day visit) lasted less than an hour. When she returned, Peggy was standing in the front yard, upset. With no explanation she had left the house, just got up and walked out through the front door and apparently stayed in the front yard until her mother returned. Carol and my client's niece, both of whom had been in the home during this time, had no explanation for what occurred either. Suddenly, they reported, Peggy just got up and left. Nothing had been said by anyone that could be identified as the cause.

"You're serious," I said, almost as a question.

"Yes... Absolutely!"

"How long ago was this? What's happened since?" Peggy left, returned home. My client phoned her daughter — several times following this inexplicable, schizophrenic drama which occurred about eight months ago. In each case her daughter's response was the same. She made it clear. She was no longer part of the family. She wanted no more association with them, none of them — no calls, letters, gifts; no communications.

#

Sometimes unusual problems arrive in pairs. Three or four weeks earlier a similar dehiscement occurred in another client's life, again, a daughter who announced her separation from the family. Its other members, all of them, were to honor her request to stay out of her life — no visits, drive-bys (because mother and daughter lived in the same city), no calls or correspondence — for any reason.

"Death included?" I asked.

"Death, too." My client was tearful. "She doesn't want to be informed even when I die."

How can this happen in people's lives? What stimulated this separation? The mother didn't know. This severance, also, was sudden, deliberate, without any cause that my client could (or would) identify. This case similarly arose out of a will interview. "Include her, too," were my instructions, however, in this case.

"If she disclaims?"

"Disclaims?"

"If she refuses the gift."

"Can she do that?"

"Yes," I answered.

"Then to her kids."

"What if she won't allow them to accept the inheritance either, or what if they refuse it?" I questioned.

She shook her head. "You're bringing up too many problems. I don't care."

"Okay, in that case... to your other children?"

"Sure," she replied.

My questions were exhausting her. I could have said anything. This mother was resolved to the reality of the separation. She didn't like it, perhaps blamed it on her daughter's social climbing, the influence of her son-in-law or his family, she didn't say, but it wasn't going to stop her from evidencing her unreciprocated love one final time. This daughter was going to get a share however small or large her mother's estate might be by then.

"Want to write her a final letter?" I asked, "...put it with the will, tell her that you love and care for her, that she's yours and always will be, that separated she's still loved?"

"Yes." She smiled. "I'll do that." And she did, brought it to the signing ceremony and clipped it to her will. The envelope was addressed to her daughter — "To Mary," it read, and it was sealed — for Mary's eyes only. With luck there will be reconciliation and the letter can be unclipped and destroyed. For her, however, such a happy event won't require a rewrite of the will. Mary's share is in it. Mary is still her mom's child and is still loved. Mom hasn't divorced her child. The will and its provisions for her disunited daughter are proof of that. Mom will have the last words. However expressed, they read, like it or not, my child, I love you.

#

A few moments passed. I broke the silence.

#

"Peggy's suffering, you know."

"What do you mean?"

"She's losing her baby sister — the one she took care of and looked after when your kids were growing up. She had to set the example, pass on her experience to her. She was the one who protected Carol, the one who heard about Carol's problems before you did, the one her baby sister confided in. Peggy was her heroine, the one she wanted to grow up and be like."

My client listened, didn't speak, but didn't look away, so I continued.

"Three and one, six and four, nine and seven — Carol could never catch up. Peggy always went through things first, didn't she? Peggy's hand-me-downs were worn by Carol, proudly — after all they had been her big sister's. Even when they had their spats their bond continued. Their love for each other and Carol's admiration of Peggy made this possible." I paused. I held my tearful client's hand.

"Peggy can't protect her anymore."

Carol is ill and Peggy is helpless — a failure in this episode. And is she alarmed by her "Thank God it isn't me?" feelings? Is this a guilt that belies her role — one given her by the order of her birth? Does she still hear her mother's voice, "Take care of Carol, Peg"? How often did her mom say that to her? First day of Carol's school — old enough to go now, a big girl in kindergarten, a word she couldn't even pronounce, so Peggy had to keep correcting her until finally it came out right. And the duty didn't end. Sixth grade and third, seventh and fourth, even though Peggy was then in junior high, in a different building — still, apart, her role remained.

Peggy and Carol were now home again — and their separate lives and homes far distanced from each other, were for the moment forgotten — children again with Mom but with Carol's young life ending. And Peggy couldn't stand the reality that her loved sister was dying. Run. Get out. Pretend it's not over, that this is not happening — flee. These were her emotions. She'd lived with them one full day in the same house with Carol again, unable to make her much loved sister's problem go away.

Carol was accommodated to her reality. Strength came from her loving husband and strong son. Peggy was addressing it in Carol's presence for the first time. Being with her sister again in their mother's house, the family home, they were children again and their lifetime bond, the foundation of their relationship was remembered — Peggy take care of Carol.... And she couldn't.

A long period of quiet passed. Neither of us spoke. There was no need to fill this needed quiet time with voice. My client's head was slightly bowed. Emotion spends our energy quickly.

Peggy needs to know that what she did — bolt, run, dash to fresh air seduced by her mind's disappointing trick to rid its body's heart of grief — is understood by her mother and certainly by her sister, who herself surely ran, bolted in her own way after the doomful announcement was first heard from her physician.

Peggy left with no goodbyes, but her leaving was not a final exit. She is not a failure. Carol is now her equal, baby sister no more. Both are women now, fully grown, with mutual care and bonded-love that no disease can forever destroy.

Carol needs to tell Peggy that she understands. That she ran, also. And that she loves her sister and needs her still.

My client left. I got a hug and kiss on the cheek at the door. Nothing else was said. We both knew — Peggy's place in Mom's will is secure. There will be reconciliation. Carol will call her big sister. She needs Peggy — one final time. Her sister's role has not changed, and she will assume it again. Her phone will ring and she will hear Carol speak, "Peg, it's Carol. I love you!"

"My Son Wanted Me To Die!"

"My son wanted me to die."

I looked at my client quizzically, and he continued. "I was in the hospital. My colon was removed; fortunately the tumor was benign." That meant, I knew — colostomy, so the tumor was only comparatively kind.

"I'm here about my will."

Retribution time, I thought; son is about to receive a pay-back.

"My son told my doctor not to resuscitate me if my heart stopped. And it did, in mid-operation, but the doctor resuscitated me anyway — and my son was angry because he did. I wasn't terminal. Why would my boy do that? Why did he want me to die?" The question wasn't directed to me. I was witnessing the introduction of a quodlibet, a philosophical monologue, an introspective search for understanding, an attempt to rescue a father's relationship with his son. There was no reason for me to speak, to defend or to excoriate his son. My role was to listen. Remaining quiet, not verbally responding, made it possible for the pother to continue. This client was resolving his own problem, resurrecting a connection with his only family member, the last of the line. His son, although married, had no children. This client continued to think out loud for thirty minutes or so. I never looked away, took no notes, but nodded appropriately, affirming conclusions that he made. By nodding I also suggested that I understood his feelings, intellectually at least, and that he should continue. This was effortful. It's easy for us to give advice, to interrupt a client's flow of words, to direct the interview to the announced subject, and to infect the conversation with our values. It's difficult to listen, often painful, but this is sometimes our role — playing psychiatrist and priest. This client needed to forgive his son, to be able to love him again.

"I'm here about my will," was euphemistic. His mission was more important, his need more urgent. He was in my office hoping that it would be possible for him to love his son again, quietly hoping that his lawyer would recognize this need.

#

"Nothing for Bobby." These were my instructions from another client this same week.

"Roberta?" I asked.

"Yeah," she answered. My client in this instance was tough, a 77-year old indecorous renegade, who talked like a blustering ruffian, forceful and profane. "She's got too damn much now," her mother said. "Comes to my house, looks around, and tells me what she wants of it when I die — and that's pretty much everything. And she's got a foul mouth." I suddenly understood the pot calling the kettle black metaphor.

"You've got three kids?" She didn't answer. I silently wondered if any of them were at all like her; it sounded like "Bobby" might be.

"Oh, what the hell," my outré client finally said, "Give her $50,000.00..." but a breath later changed her mind. "What if that's more than the others get?"

"You've got $481,000.00 today in cash, plus your home. That's what your statement shows. It's unlikely, but it could happen, I suppose — what about $50,000.00 or twenty per cent, whichever is greater? Twenty per cent gives the others eighty per cent, forty each, twice as much to your other daughters." Is this punishment enough for being too much like you, too much a swashbuckler, I wondered?

"Do your kids get along?"

"Damned if I know," she replied, "They're out of the house; I suppose so."

I don't believe I've ever had a client who cussed so much. I could see her in the local tavern swilling down the suds, entertaining the crowd. She surely entertained me. It was her *persona*. And I bet her kids are all tough, too — all three. I think she loves her kids, but I'm not sure. Her heart was certainly not into will-making. If her attitude demonstrated love of children, it certainly was masked by her demeanor. What a contrast to the client in my office now.

#

"What should I do?" This was the final sentence of his long, emotive diatribe. Now he was quiet; he seemed spent. He consumed a lot of energy confronting his emotions — aloud and in the presence of his lawyer. This was an important moment for him — I'd heard the story, now what punishment might be fashioned in this new will that will serve as a message to his callous son? And it was now my turn to speak.

"You love your son, don't you, Alex." This was a statement of recognition by me, not a question to him. I continued, "Set aside this episode for a moment. Tell me about your boy." So he did. I was mistaken about my client's energy being spent. Twenty minutes passed, a new and intimate monologue had begun. He told me about his son's birth, and how he and his wife brought their infant home from the hospital. Alex carried his young son, his only descendant, held carefully in his arms, into the family home where my client still lives. The young boy weighed just over seven pounds — in diapers, Alex recalled. He was 22 inches long. Length changes to short or tall, I believe, once an infant becomes upright and can stand erect against a prominent door frame for the periodic measurement where the pencil mark impression and date written in small print on the paint is made. Those marks were still on Alex's kitchen door frame. "I'll never paint over them," he said.

I thought of other door frames I'd seen in clients' homes. They're all the same, precious, unerasable time lines. He talked to his fresh little critter and told his small, newlyborn boy, his only child as it turned out, that he loved him and that "I always will." It was obvious to me that he still did — and always would. Son's mistake in judgment was being forgiven.

New will, okay, my friend, I thought, my turn to speak again, so I asked, "What do you want the new will to say?" I had a copy of his current will on the table before me. I took out a red felt tip pen. The changes made in red on the redraft are going to stand out.

"Well," my client answered, "there are three young boys, grandchildren of friends of mine. I don't think that they're well off. The boys are ten or eleven. I'd like to give $10,000.00 to each of them to help with their education."

"How much do you have?" I asked. He looked at his notes, pulling them from his right inside coat pocket. "$123,868.13," he said. He knew to the penny.

"Son get's the balance?"

"Of course," he affirmed with an emphasis that suggested, "How could you think otherwise?"

Punishment completed; son forgiven.

"And if son predeceases you?"

"His wife" — same as in the prior will, an uncommon reaction. "My child's okay but he's adversely influenced by his spouse," is a more common theme, but not for Alex. His son's wife wasn't blamed for this event.

Alex owned other assets as well. The $123,868.13 was just the value of his current cash accounts. He owns his home. Value? $125,914.87. This was really strange, an idiosyncracy. He had everything valued down to the penny. This house value was taken from the county tax assessor's report. So the home was probably worth more, but the county value for the moment was good enough for him. The home would go to his son, also, no different from Alex's prior plan.

A few other details were attended to and then he stood up. Two hours had passed, and he was tired.

"Hey," he said, "I'd like you to meet my boy."

"I'd like that. Why don't we three meet here when it's convenient and talk about what your son should do if you get sick again. You can tell him what you want him to do if there's a next time. We can see if he's comfortable with that, and you can ask if he'd like a mate so joint decisions could be made, less pressure on your boy than if he has to make critical decisions alone."

"I'd like that. I like the 'mate' idea. I'll call you."

I'm eager about our next meeting. I think I'll like Alex's boy, who now, of course, is in middle age, but is still his child. I know a lot about him now — a hundred twenty minutes' worth — and I sure do like his dad!

"It's All My Money!"

"It's all my money!" Her statement was made with emphasis. She meant it, and anyone challenging her opinion, including her husband, it was clear, would be met with more than mild argument.

"And what do you own?" I asked her solemn and docile husband.

"He spent his!" She answered for him. The Colonel made no reply. He was po-faced. He didn't resist his wife's assessment about ownership. But why should he? This isn't a conference about marriage termination. The couple, married nearly 60 years, were updating their wills. "It's all my money," was Mrs. Peabody's response to the lawyer's question. "What do you two own?"

One million! That was the total of the long list of numerous accounts, a few payable on death to the couple's children, but the majority of the money this pair had saved were in the Mrs. accounts — her name alone, to be ultimately distributed by the terms of her will.

She was a short, podgy lady, the Colonel's wife; her pretty hair swept upward on the sides and back made her look taller than she actually was. She was well dressed and she wore high heels. They looked new. This meeting with the lawyer was obviously an important occasion for them.

Mrs. Peabody's husband was quiet, his complexion rather gray — not a healthful sign. He appeared tired, energyless, and any verbal reply from him was extravasated. I had to specifically address him. His replies had to be forced, and even then, his wife would intervene and answer for him, or confirm or challenge what he had to say.

This was a curious, antipodean couple. He quietly tolerated what appeared to be visceral control of this couples' decision-making by his wife, and offered no resistance, even when I spoke directly to him and asked, "Do you agree?" This union had two parties but one had no voice. The Colonel was definitely a limited partner in his relationship with his wife.

"One million — all in your name," I said, looking at the Colonel's wife. "Interested in saving some estate tax?" She was, although she looked quizzically at me — which I understood to mean, "Don't mess with *my* money." I explained how the assets could be divided so that there would be no estate tax until the survivor of them died and in all probability, none then, either. The division of their assets to create this savings didn't even need to be equal. She could control sixty per cent and he forty, and that percentage could change each year as the increased federal estate tax exemption rose.

"That's hardly fair," she responded when I drew out on paper a diagram of how the savings could be very simply and economically accomplished, but its ownership could no longer be solitary, no longer exclusively hers. She would have to share. "It's all my money. He spent his," was her response to the tax-saving diagram. "What did he spend it on?" I asked. As it turned out, he paid the bills normally and naturally incurred by families — rent, utilities, family cars, furnishings, the kids' schooling, food, family vacations. There was nothing singularly personal on her list of what I thought might be extravagances benefitting him alone. All of the paychecks not spent in this way, Mrs. Peabody had at some point transferred into her personal savings accounts. She had them scattered out all over the city and a big one at the Ft. Sam Houston Bank, a mainstay financial institution for all retired military officers and their spouses. The accounts were all in her name alone and they now totaled one million dollars. Some saver the Colonel's wife, if she in fact accomplished this feat alone. There had to be some inheritance, but the source of this wealth was unimportant. She was convinced that whatever its source — it was hers.

"The federal estate tax will be $150,000.00, actually $153,800 this year on a million dollars," I explained to her again, but she changed the subject.

"My breakfront," she said, "it's full to the hilt."

"Filled with what?" I asked.

"Well, china and silver. I have a large punch bowl with cups that hang on the side, several sets of china and flatware. And I have jewelry," (but probably not in the breakfront, I quietly surmised).

"Okay," I said, "then the tax will be higher. Forty-one per cent minimum (over your one million dollars) times the value of your personal items. What are they worth?"

"Lots," she answered. Tax at death was apparently not a sufficient reason in her mind to title the one million in separate investment accounts — some in hers, some in his.

Something is wrong here, I knew. This isn't normal. I was worried about the Colonel's health. His graying facial color is unnatural, and my friend is nearing eighty. Could the grayness mean lack of oxygen and heart problems, I wondered, so I asked.

"How's your health, Colonel?" I looked directly at him.

"He's fine," his wife too quickly answered. "And yours, Mrs. P, your health, how is it?"

"There's nothing wrong with me." But she didn't say — *either*, "There's nothing wrong with me — *either*." It appeared to me that Mrs. P's responding to all questions asked of them — even those asked directly and solely of her husband — was protective of him because he is declining. Mrs. P might not even be aware of her guardian-like behavior.

Could it be that she is anticipating his death and this is why the assets are all now alone in her name — much if not all of the family's resources transferred into her separate accounts only recently because she is anticipating his death, simplifying the estate, eliminating joint accounts, assuming that this is a way of avoiding probate, something, perhaps, she believes she must, for unknown reasons, do.

"How long have the assets been in your name alone?" I asked, looking now at Mrs. Peabody. "I don't know." There was a long pause — "awhile," she finally said unconvincingly.

Confirmed! Her homemade estate plan is in operation: put all assets in the name of the survivor *before* she becomes that — before she becomes the grieving widow. And she's in her lawyer's office now to receive his blessing. She wants to hear an "all is well, my child," confirmation that what she's done is okay.

"When was your last physical, Colonel?" They both answered, a chorus with each speaking different words, but the meaning was the same — it had been a long time.

"How long have we known each other? Do you remember?" Mrs. P reached into her satchel and pulled out their first wills. I had done them thirty years ago. They were simple wills, no trusts, "John loves Mary" type documents, leaving everything to each other, alternatively to their children. "Did I really draft these things?" I wondered. They were awful, or at best not very good, written on 14-inch long paper, filled with lawyers' words. The wills began, "Know All Men By These Presents...." The first letter of each word in this prelude was capitalized affirming in this more enlightened age the sexism of the 1960s, and uncomfortably, perhaps an unconscious bias of the drafter of the documents in that age as well.

"Thirty years ago — that's when we first met? But I've written your wills since then, several times."

"Yes," the Colonel spoke again, softly, effortfully, "and we've saved them — all of them." They were in the satchel, too, a series of documents written over our long history. Folded and held together by large rubber bands, Mrs. Peabody laid them on the table. I left them where they lay. These documents were not important. They were no longer relevant to this couple's needs.

I put my hands on Mrs. P's hands. She had them clasped on the table.

I spoke to them both. "Will you two do a favor for me?"

They didn't answer, just looked at me. Their look, particularly the Colonel's, was, "of course; tell us what it is." "Before you return for a second visit here — which you'll need to do, the hour's up and I know that this conversation has been tiring — get physicals. Get checked out. You can do this at Ft. Carson, can't you?" Carson is the local Army base and in the Colorado Springs community retirees form a steady stream on the state highway leading to its health care facilities and pharmacy. I removed my grip on Mrs. P's hands. I looked at her unlively and vimless husband. I was blunt. "Colonel, I don't like your color. Your cheeks aren't rosy. Will you do this for me? And do it for your two daughters also, and for each other. Then come back. Your planning problems are relatively simple. We can fix up your legal stuff in short order. Okay?"

"Okay," they both agreed, and there was at least moderate enthusiasm in their voices. "We will."

I watched them leave, hanging on to each other, shuffling a bit, taking short, unquick steps; their feet weren't lifted more than a few millimeters from the floor, inviting any loose rug edge to cause a fall. But they made it to the elevator and we said our goodbys there, again. I wondered, then, if I'd done the right thing. I'm not a physician. Was this suggestion — get physicals — an invasion of their privacy? Should I have said, "Your cheeks aren't rosy?" Is my job to do as I'm told — write wills the way the clients direct after the options are explained to them and any conflicts I have, disclosed? Am I to assume that the earned income is not "all my money," when I get no argument from the companion-spouse? Is my role scrivener alone?

#

About a year ago another client made an appointment for a review of her will. I'd known her for a long time also. She was a realtor and sold the first home that my wife and I built in Stratmoor Hills, a subdivision in the highlands of southwest Colorado Springs when we moved from there. She was a Christian Scientist and had been a member of the Colorado Springs Christian Science church nearly all of her life. Seldom ill, she consulted a journaled practitioner when health care was an issue. On her most recent visit, however, she wore a high-necked blouse, up to her chin, similar to a turtleneck sweater, but even this could not hide the massive swelling on one side and on the entire front of her neck. This distortion made her nearly unrecognizable to me. On her left cheek was a black and red swollen area, the size of a half-dime. A pinkish shade of red encircled the melanoma in strong contrast to her pale cheeks. The discoloration was the size of a half-dollar.

She didn't mention her appearance nor any illness. My instructions were to revise her will, include her son, her only child, as beneficiary. Finally, after thirty years of redrafted wills, each one affirming his disinheritance, he was now to be included, the principal beneficiary. Her peace with him near in time to her unspoken but stoic recognition of her own mortality was finally accomplished.

I rewrote her will, never mentioning in our conversation her clearly apparent tumor and the neon melanoma beneath her eye.

What is my responsibility, I wondered, in this case, also. I called a physician, a friend of mine, the local coroner. "She's dead," he replied, when I described her appearance to him. "It's too late to help her. She'll eventually choke to death unless she dies sooner. The epithelial carcinoma can't be reversed now. She's in the end-stage."

It's easy, of course, to make such a conclusion on the phone with a faceless patient and no one around who can overhear. It was unpleasant, but direct, clear, concise passing of information from one professional to another. "Your client's dead." But what if,

I wondered, the illness wasn't at end-stage yet — perhaps just the reddish-black facial melanoma appearing, no swollen tumor. Should I inquire then, urge my client to see someone about the preface to a tump, the growth that will follow, sealing her fate? My clients are my friends. Am I to remain silent, play the game, by pretending not to notice, act as if nothing is wrong?

#

I took what I hope is the high road with Colonel Peabody. With him, with any luck, it won't be too late, and he can get help. I'm waiting for the call. The silence is discomforting and burdensome to me. It's been seventeen days since I bid my friends goodbye. So far the second appointment has not been made — and I know it may never be.

"Your Move, Andy"

He is a millionaire, maybe a zillionaire. In all events, he's got a lot of money, a lot of land, too. And he's a cowboy, a rancher. During the day, at least, he's always in his leather boots, the real thing, not tourist boots shown off in merchants' windows appealing to the city's guests, ones vacationing here who walk the main avenue in my town, looking for things that they can take home and show off to their friends. The cowboys, like my zillionaire friend, have their own shop where the real western stuff is sold. My friend and all those like him buy all their stuff there — Wranglers® and wide brims, thick belts with large buckles and wide braces which they still call suspenders.

The sun has wizened their faces and they're wrinkled from working all day in the sun, real cowboy work out with the animals and in the fields.

They're serious people; they love their vocation and a lot of them are wealthy, like my client here who has just ambled in. He's got a strange rocking motion when he walks made necessary by his large-heeled boots and his permanently stooped posture caused by years of hard work "on the place," his ranch where he personally works the herd and the horses, a moral necessity ingrained in him and working ranchers generally. They are free spirits; they speak their mind and you can trust them with your life. They are solid people, men and women of the earth.

My client, one of them, sat in the conference room, occupying the same chair he always uses. His C.P.A. sat at the table's end and I sat across from our client. Andy, we called him, Andrew Caine.

He squinted at me. "Are them — what do ya' call them — wife agreements! Are they any good?"

Andy is in his mid-80's. "Getting married?" I asked, wondering whom the woman might be and how he had met her.

"I'm considerin' my options. I can't pass the damn driving test — license is up — end of May — my eyes."

"You're looking for a driver?"

"Yeah."

"Hire one."

"That don't work."

"Really?"

"Can't count on 'em."

"You're going to get married so you'll have someone to drive you around?"

"Maybe."

She must be young, I thought. "Well, to answer your question, Andy, the agreements work — at least when they're fair and when they're well-written. Why don't you have a sit-down with a divorce lawyer. Your C.P.A. and I can give you a name — or several names if you want. They know the problems; they have to defend the agreements or try to void them. Hear what a matrimonial lawyer advises. Then make your decision. And if you decide to marry, then get the agreement written. Her lawyer will need to approve it — and that lawyer won't if it's not reasonable and fair."

There was no response. Perhaps he didn't like the "maybe" answer, the somewhat tentative "it depends" response. We were together, the three of us, at this time to sign a will and a private foundation we'd set up for him — a year in the process. He's not swift, in no hurry and if it's a driver he wants, he won't need her until the end of May — 2 months away, lots of time to chew and spit tobacco and think about what this chauffeur might ultimately cost him. So the conversation about marriage stopped. It would be his first; he'd never married. He's in for a shock if he does. But he can handle himself. He's smart — wealthy, unflappable, king of his ranch, and his four-legged subjects. It might be a kick. Perhaps I've done all I need to do here. Is there any reason I should be negative? The chauffeur ploy may be the public reason to marry — perhaps he's found somebody he cares about as much as his livestock and now, finally, is ready to discover what commitment to another human being means in real life.

"Your move, Andy."

Postscript

Marrying, having children and dying, these events are much about money — earning it, saving it, sharing it and disposing of it. "Ellen" illustrates this as well as the last four essays ending with "Your Move, Andy" (Chapter 21).

Lawyers who listen to older clients hear stories about the difficulty of sharing wealth. That's the unspoken issue which Andy faces in whether or not to marry in order to get a reliable chauffeur. The continued independence his vehicle gives him, which he will lose when his license will no longer be renewed — what's that worth in money which he'll need to share when he opens his bachelor—home to his new chauffeur—wife.

The will we just wrote will be changed. His commitment to his driver will be read on double—spaced lines in computer type, not an untidy self—interested scrawl hurriedly written on a handy lined tablet, a free item made available to its customers by the local feed store. His life will change and there won't be a disinheritance. The chauffeur's lawyer will see to that.

Peggy's illness and Alex's frustration with his son momentarily altered their views about wealth transmission. The colonel's wife won't change. The money's hers; she's keeping it, and Andy Caine is about to receive a lesson in what sharing wealth means in real life. It's all in a day's work for an elder lawyer.

PART SEVEN

...With No Tide and No One to Push

"I feel like a beached whale." Audry's assessment was accurately metaphoric for her physical condition, too. Her lower limbs are useless, her right arm and hand fully immobile. And now, she is explaining to me, that her ability to use her left hand and arm is diminishing, numbing, becoming useless, also. Soon her Multiple Sclerosis will make her fully quadriplegic. The use of her body's physical extensions, making it possible to deal with her world, small as her environment has become, will be gone. Her limbs will be paralyzed; she will be helpless, fully dependent.

Audry lies on her right side, periodically needing to be moved to avoid bedsores, injuries she can't feel when her skin ulcerates, but she can still reach her water glass, drink through a straw unaided and manipulate the TV channel.

Once positioned in her motorized wheelchair, which she calls her "Chevy," she can move through the nursing home hallways, steering with her still usable left forearm and hand, and talk to her friends. With her engaging and uncomplaining personality, her friends are just about everyone who lives and works in the home.

While she can read, she has no way to hold a book; she can no longer write, turn herself or control her body. She has to be carefully strapped erect in her "Chevy." If she leans and her weight shifts, she can't right herself and the mobile chair could tip. She's trapped in an unresponsive and unforgiving body — no way out — no escape.

I met Audry several months ago when her husband died. He was her caregiver. A man comparatively small in size, his heart wore out. He was her body's extension, and made it possible for her to remain in her home. Observing and imagining all that he was required to do for her, her description of him as "a saint," certainly fit. His enlarged portrait, a photograph of a handsome man with trimmed moustache and close-cropped hair, dashing really, in his military uniform and sergeant stripes, hangs on the wall to her left, the wall she rather constantly faces. In this form he remains with her, and she can imagine him present, watching over her; and she can talk to him.

Audry lies in a bed in a West Side Colorado Springs nursing home. Private pay for now, she has a small but private room that looks out to the main corridor. Activity up and down that wide hallway throughout the day gives her something to look at. Like teenagers when many of us were growing up, before there were malls, and with little else to do and no money to spend, parking on the cities' main streets in the early evening to watch the parade up and down the Ave'. The kids peered at the window shoppers and others who were just out for a walk amid the evening's quiet activity. It was free entertainment for the teen crowd who had access to the family sedan and who had spent their last bucks on gas. Similar to the city's main street and the somewhat mundane activity that the teens observed there, is Audry's corridor, her car's window — an opportunity to see who, in their own way, is strutting down her Ave'. She gets to watch and she never tires of this daily Circus. She sees new faces, new doctors and old ones, new admitees being pushed in wheelchairs, sometimes families, and little children being told to "be quiet," by their noisy parents. Her corridor, not routine, is a scene of lively action, activity she loves to watch. It is a stimulating counterpoint to her personal condition.

"What's up, Aud'?" I asked as I entered her somewhat darkened room.

"I want to give my house to my son," she replied.

This is our usual routine. I say hello. She responds with the same command softened only by the preface, "I want...."

"The one in prison?" I ask, knowing that she has only one son surviving, but it's part of our shtick.

"Yes, you know that."

"You told me he's into drugs — in prison for pushing."

"He's clean now."

"He's in prison. Aud', of course, he's clean." Having worked in Norfolk Prison, in Walpole, Massachusetts, while a student at Boston University, I said this with slight tongue-in-cheek. She laughed. So did I.

Her room lights were out. The TV was on. I'd caught her in a somewhat groggy state — waking up from what she described as "a doze." But she knew that it was her lawyer and she played the game. We both have the patter down just right.

It was 6:00 p.m. — about meal time for Audry. Dining is not abysmally early where Audry resides as it is in some nursing homes. When the tray arrives, I can help her eat. She knows that. It is an effort for her because I lack good bedside feeding skills. But she always laughingly tolerates the clumsiness and excuses the aide who brings in the tray. "The *maitre d'* will 'serve'," she says, and the $5.50-per-hour guy leaves. Audry always makes it seem as though I am doing her a great service. But we get to talking and I forget to scoop up the food and hold it up so she can ingest it. The aide, I think, finishes up after I leave. At that point, though, I think the "dining" stops and she just eats. She knows there's a difference. While I'm there with the plate and spoon, it gives Audry and me a chance to talk without focusing just on legal stuff.

Now energized, she's back on the attack.

"Well, he's my only son now. I'm his mother."

Audry lost a son several years earlier — the favored one — the good one. Much like his father, his heart failed, too — twenty years sooner than his dad's. The felon's heart, however, works just fine, but since junior high — seventh grade — he's been into drugs — a user, and to support his need, a seller as well.

#

"What will he do with the house, Aud'?" I asked. It was a duplex that earns rental income for her, an asset that could extend her private-pay status in a care center for several years.

"Well," she assumed that once out of the State Correctional Institution that, "he'd live in it."

And perhaps he would. And mother's highest expectation for him would be realized. But I can't take that chance.

"Audry, you'll be out of funds in a few years; then you'll need Medicaid. No private room. No room on the Ave'."

"I don't care about me," she interrupted.

I paused a moment — timing is important... "Your son does," I said, hoping that I was right, because at age 38, he's been in trouble more often than not.

And then there was quiet.

She's playing mom. That's her role. Her son is still a child, her child. Caring for him is the right thing for her to do. It's an honest emotion. She may blame herself for his condition, his weakness, his lack of self-esteem, and for what will likely be his too-soon death.

She needs to know that one who is a son worthy of family membership cares and would not take a resource from her that would make her mind and soul's entrapment in her useless body an even worse experience. Giving him the home would result in her being reassigned sooner to a room in the asylum's back corridor where distressed and destitute individuals are housed, where the shrieks of mindless bodies cry out during all waking hours for help. The moaning from these tombs are pitiful sounds, reflecting anguish that accompanies the over-populated bedrooms in the Medicaid wards — the home's section where few bodies move up and down their Ave'.

"Your son cares! — Want to test this, Audry? Shall we offer him the home, tell him the consequence to you? Because I will. Shall we see if he is still a taker, not yet a man?

Shall we see if he is like his soldier-father — one who sees others' needs and joins in to help, one who sacrifices? Is he one who thinks first of you — his only priority in truth — the last of the family who can help you in your survival of Life without a body to do its work?"

I hadn't been quite this direct with Audry before. But now I sensed that it was necessary. The game's over, at least for today. It's time now to be serious. At stake is the necessary comfort of an anguished soul.

There was silence.

"Keeping the house means several more years of private pay," Audry finally acknowledged, "but I don't want to live that long. And I can't do suicide." I thought she meant — physically, she couldn't, but that was obvious; she continued:

"Not suicide — because I don't know what's on the other side."

I left the metaphysical line alone. Suicide isn't an issue anyway. There's no way that she can do herself in — a "beached whale" — her description, with no tide and no one to push.

Wanting or not wanting to live is not the issue, at least not today, but if she does live, her lawyer's role is to see to her comfort, to insure that her property is not recklessly wasted by a prodigal, a wanderer who has returned and cashes in once again, using mom and her mixture of love and guilt to get his fix, his momentary pleasure.

The conversation is exhausting. It tires us both. It will continue. The opening lines will be the same. What follows will be determined by Audry. It won't be adversarial; it never is. She knows my role and benefits by it. I won't give in. Son will get no deed stroked by my pen. She knows that. But she can still be mom, still be caring, still be hopeful, still be loving to her remaining flesh and blood. She can face her own guilt by ordering me to give the last of her possessions to one I consider to be lavish wastrel — safely knowing that I won't — that I will protect her — that I will play the role of dutiful son, the role she cannot trust her own child to play. It's our game. She's a bright lady.

She knows that I am aware of her motivation, and I know that she knows that I will not be seduced into jeopardizing her necessary care in the final years of her near hopeless life.

#

It was late when I arrived at home, after seven o'clock. "How was work today, Honey?" my wife asked, as she removed the tantalizing baked Salmon from the oven, its flavor accentuated with lemon juice, salt-free soy, herbs and olive oil. It was my turn now to be looked after. "Fine," I replied, "same as always."

*Ad Litem — Ad Letem**

What is the correct pronunciation of the legal term *ad litem*? That's Latin, as we know, meaning, "for the suit,"[1] used regularly as a term of art in cases where *guardian ad litems* are appointed to protect parties who are incapacitated by infancy or otherwise. In Latin such persons are called *defensors*, temporary and important *custos, praeses, curators*. They are defenders of their charges.[2]

The Latin uses the letter "i" both as a consonant, pronounced like the English "y," and as a vowel. Using the Latin "i" as a consonant, for example, results in the word, Iam, meaning now or already, being pronounced, yam. The "i" is given a "y" sound.

Latin uses the same letter as a vowel, and each Latin vowel has a long and a short version. The short "i" is heard in our word dip; the long vowel is obvious in our word, deep, resulting in a strong "e" sound.[3]

The Latin word *litem*, properly spoken, uses the long vowel, and is therefore, pronounced, leetem.

The Honorable E. David Griffith, Magistrate of the Probate Court in El Paso County, Colorado, with sensitive deference to the lawyers who are privileged to appear in his court with their clients, takes his cues from counsel. If a lawyer uses litem, emphasizing the harsh "i" sound, so does the judge — but he knows better.

In a recent conversation with a retired and highly regarded jurist, the Magistrate was told that the Latin, *litem*, had been Americanized, and the vowel with the strong "i" sound is now culturally appropriate. Perhaps the jurist is correct, and we have befallen to those who have forced a worsened word upon us.[4]

Patricia L. Harrison[5], an elder law practitioner, was appointed as a guardian ad litem, made defender, the *custos* for an elder male schizophrenic who had been a resident of Crafts Farrow State Hospital in Columbia, South Carolina for 13 years. She has taken her appointment seriously. Allegedly incompetent to transact his own business affairs, and eight days before he was involuntarily committed to a state institution in 1954,6 relatives had her charge execute a deed to them transferring property in which he had an interest on what is now the cloverleaf for Interstate 26 in Orangeburg, South Carolina.[7] On July 11, 1954, just one week after the deed was dated, the affected person was involuntarily committed to a state psychiatric hospital with a diagnosis of "chronic brain disorder."[8]

A conservator, the ward's mother, was ultimately appointed by the court for her son because he was believed to be incapacitated. This didn't occur, however, until 1975, and

* This chapter is endnoted. The notes can be found at the end of this chapter.

a co-fiduciary, the sister of the ward, was appointed to jointly serve in this capacity seven years later, in July 1982. The court made this joint-appointment without a due process hearing and without notice to anyone. Twelve years after the original fiduciary appointment, the ward's mother resigned as conservator, and a second relative, a niece of the disabled person, was approved by the court as a co-conservator and co-guardian. Such subsequent appointment was also made ex parte, and without notice to the incapacitated and aging ward.[9]

While the net worth of the affected pupillus[10] exceeded one million dollars, Patricia Harrison reports,[11] when she was made guardian ad litem, the fiduciaries' court reports accounted for less than $100,000.00 of his assets. On Harrison's request, the Court ordered a complete accounting. That amended financial disclosure filed by the conservators failed to report more than $200,000.00 held by the fiduciaries in certificates of deposit.

Repeated recommendations in 1982 and 1983 for the ward's release were made by the hospital where the incapacitated person had been placed. An anticipated release that was to occur in October 1983 was inexplicably stopped.[12] Finally, in April 1994, thirteen years after his last involuntary hospitalization, the court ordered that continued state hospital confinement was no longer required for Patricia's charge.[13] The parties had agreed in March 1994 that conditions no longer existed to warrant his continued confinement in the state mental institution, but his discharge was delayed by the then-conservators. They had been previously appointed by the court without notice, without hearings and without legal representation for the one allegedly demented, but they refused to execute the documents necessary to effect his liberation from Crafts Farrow. That requirement was not formally satisfied until eleven months after the patient's release from the mental institution was judicially ordered.[14]

The non-lawyer judge, whose court controlled the protected person's file, held at least one private meeting with an interested party in the case, a prominent South Carolina politician-lawyer, who represented the co-conservators. Such meeting was discovered by the guardian ad litem because the conservators' lawyer billed for it, and the court authorized payment. Another *ex parte* meeting between the court and the conservators' lawyer was actually tape recorded and transcribed.[15]

The guardian ad litem was chastised by the court because she had taken her pupillus to a private psychiatrist for examination. This was done by Patricia in response to the conservators' attorney's request that he be allowed to unilaterally select physicians to examine the protected person.

Our colleague, Patricia L. Harrison, asked the court to recuse itself, or to allow a venue change. She had filed a lawsuit against the South Carolina Department of Mental Health, the employer of the judge's niece. The best interest of the ward demanded recusal, evidenced by the lack of due process, including solo conferences with counsel for the conservators and *ex parte* hearings. In response, the Orangeburg County Probate Court Judge, with no notice of its intent to terminate the guardian ad litem, with no testimony, nor findings of fact concerning how removal might adversely affect the ward's interest, and without cause removed Patricia Harrison as *custos, praeses*, as *curator*, as guardian "for the suit" of her charge.[16]

And Patricia has responded. She has faced her adversary — the court itself — on behalf of one she is mandated by appointment and conscience to protect. The National Academy of Elder Law Attorneys (NAELA) is helping her — an *amicus* (long vowel) brief has been filed with the appellate court.

Our country can be proud of the National Academy of Elder Law Attorneys. NAELA lawyers go where their clients are hurting and at the time of the writing of this episode, it's in a small county in South Carolina. And it doesn't really matter if the court or anyone else pronounces our heroine's *ad litem* title with a long "e" sound or not.

ENDNOTES TO AD LITEM — AD LETEM

1. *Black's Law Dictionary*, 6th ed., (1992), p. 43. "For the suit; for the purposes of the suit; pending the suit, "aèd làytam."
2. *The Pocket Oxford Latin Dictionary*, ed., James Morwood, Oxford Univ. Press, (1994), pp. 38, 107, 233.
3. *See* "Guide to Pronunciation," *supra* n. 1, p. vi; see also H. W. Fowler, *A Dictionary of Modern English Usage*, (Oxford Un. Press, 1965, 1991 reprint), "Latin phrases", p. 324-25. The Common Law of England is the law of Colorado. *See* 2-4-211 C.R.S. That statute reads, "The common law of England, so far as the same is applicable and of a general nature, and all acts and statutes of the British parliament, made in aid of or to supply the defects of the common law prior to the fourth year of James the First, excepting the second section of the sixth chapter of forty—third Elizabeth, the eighth chapter of thirteenth Elizabeth, and the ninth chapter of thirty-seventh Henry the Eighth, and which are of a general nature, and not local to that kingdom, shall be the rule of decision, and shall be considered as of full force until repealed by legislative authority." Respecting the common law tradition which we recognize even in this century, perhaps the historic language of the law ought to be similarly accorded the respect of its own, unique voice.
4. Worsened words typically mean that the word in question has adapted to a change in meaning. Here, we have worsened the meaning of "worsened word," to now include worsened pronunciations. *See* H. W. Fowler, *A Dictionary of Modern English Usage*, 2d ed., Oxford Un. Press, (1965), p. 718.
5. This article is in large measure, a Paean, a song of praise and triumph, to this NAELA lawyer who is taking her commitment to caring for those among us who are disabled and in want, responsibly.
6. The now 70-year-old ward was hospitalized at South Carolina State Hospital in 1954, released and rehospitalized in 1964 to 1965; and hospitalized once again in 1973 for seven months. Exact dates and time periods are not reflected in the "Sociocultural History and Assessment" of the patient prepared by the senior social work supervisor who signed the 1983 report. *See Appendix of Petitioner . . ., infra* n. 8, pp. 346-347.
7. A portion of this property which was, we believe, gratuitously transferred to his relatives by the ward was sold by his brother to the state, and on which is now located Orangeburg-Calhoun Technical College.
8. The deed bore the date July 3, 1954, a Sunday; the notarization was dated a month later. The grantor had been previously hospitalized and received electroshock treatments six years earlier, in 1948, at Edgewood Sanitorium. "Chronic brain disorder," was the diagnosis reported by the GAL in correspondence with the author. The

diagnostic impression of the staff psychiatrist on May 4, 1982, was "mental retardation." The ward was then 56 years of age. *See In State of So. Carolina, In the Supreme Court, Patricia L. Harrison, as GAL v. Orangeburg County Probate Court*, Probate Case No. 83-GC-0019 (May 15, 1995), *Appendix of Petitioner for Writ of Prohibition or Other Appropriate Relief*, p. 349.

9. In August, 1994, following an accounting ordered by the court, Patricia Harrison filed a petition with the court asking that the conservators for her ward be removed for breach of fiduciary duty. In response, they submitted their resignations. As of the date of the submission of this article, petitions for hearings on the appointment of permanent fiduciaries remain pending. Other related matters are also pending.
10. A masculine ward.
11. See John Hellprin, "Accusations fly in McLean case," *Charleston Post and Courier* (May 24, 1995). *Appendix of Petitioner, supra* n. 8, p. 247; Gene Crider, "Attorney to fight her dismissal from ex-mental patient's case," *Charleston Post* . . ., (May 25, 1995), *id. Appendix, id.* p. 248; Ricki Morell, "Farmer Files Suit . . . ," *Appendix, Id.*, pp. 246, 255.
12. Hospital employees have now acknowledged that the discharge of Patricia's client was prevented by political intervention. *See* Appendix, *supra* n. 8, pp. 85, 86, 127, and 128.
13. At least 24 times between 1982 and 1994 . . . the [hospital's] treatment team recommended that [the patient be released to live in a] . . . supervised boarding home, or in some less restrictive setting . . . ." Ricki Morell, "Farmer files suit but he won't get 13 years back," *Charlotte Observer and Post*, (May 3, 1995), p. A-10, *Appendix, supra* n. 8, p. 246.
14. Originally appointed to represent the ward on February 24, 1994, Patricia Harrison, GAL, had limited authority, only to represent her charge in the proceeding to appoint a successor guardian. On April 27, 1994, the date that the court ordered her ward's release the scope of her authority was expanded. McLean's formal discharge occurred eleven months after his release was ordered. He was, however, allowed to return to his home on a hospital pass eight months after the hearing when the powers of the court—appointed fiduciaries were removed. Between March 22, 1994 and October, 1994, the fiduciaries refused to execute the documents necessary for his release.
15. Patricia Harrison discovered this private meeting when the court's own reporter called her to see if Patricia's private court reporter had transcribed the hearing held on April 22, 1994. Patricia had not been informed of a hearing on that date. She discovered that the judge had held an *ex parte* conference with the politician-lawyer who represented the co-conservators, his clients, and the South Carolina

Department of Mental Health. Five minutes of the tape had been erased. Patricia had met with her ward in Columbia on April 22, 1994. The hospital records do not indicate that he left the hospital to go to Orangeburg, yet the transcript has him listed as having attended the conference.

16. This action is contrary to the court's personal duty to insure that rights of a protected person, such as due process (fundamental fairness), are not violated. *See Cumbie v. Cumbie*, 245 SC 107, 139 S.E.2d, 477 (1964) cited in NAELA's brief. The court failed to appoint a successor G.A.L. to protect the interests of the alleged incapacitated person notwithstanding that there remain serious, unresolved issues pending before the court, relating to the administration of the ward's estate and the failure of his relative and self—interested fiduciaries to protect his best interests, and to protect his estate. *See* Motion for Leave to File an Amicus Curiae Brief, Court of Common Pleas, Civil Action No. 95-CP-38-328, Case No. 83-GC-300019, County of Orangeburg, In Re James Lennon McLean, Jr., Protected Person; *see also* n. 9.

Postscript

"God Does Work Wondrous Things" (see Chapter 7) illustrates that elder, ill individuals often need a protector. In situations where no caring child is available to play this role and no guardian has yet been appointed by the court, and no responsible agent has been given a durable power of attorney enabling her or him to act for the disabled and needful elder, the elder lawyer may be impelled to look out for her or his client's best interests. "With No Tide..." and "Ad Litem — Ad Letem," both demonstrate this need.

The American Bar Association's (A.B.A.) *Model Rules for Professional Conduct*, Model Rule 1.14, authorize attorney intervention in situations where a client's conduct puts the elder or his or her property in jeopardy. Lawyers who work with older, disabled persons are familiar with this somewhat paternalistic, but humanly necessary rule. (The rule is illustrated in A.B.A., Formal Opinion 96-404 (Aug. 2, 1996), *Annot. Model Rules of Prof. Conduct*, 3d ed., ABA (Chicago, Ill., 1996).

PART EIGHT

"Well, He Doesn't Come Home Anymore"

"My husband wants a divorce."

My client was a petite, well-groomed and attractive lady in her mid-70's. Her tone was matter of fact, business-ike, superficially unemotional, a "let's get this over with," no nonsense approach to her problem. Of course she was hurting, putting up a brave front, seeing a lawyer because that's what one does when the announcement of such an ectomy arrives; and she was acting as adult and mature about the emotional rent that she now faced, and which would surely radically influence her remaining life, as she could.

"How long have you been married to your husband?" I asked.

"Fifty years," she replied.

"How old is he?"

"Seventy-five."

"And you?"

"I'm seventy-five also."

She used *also* rather than, *too*. Her grammar was impressive and I surmised that I was dealing with an educated client here; that will help.

"Why," I asked, "does he want a divorce?"

"He's found someone he wants to marry."

#

Her answers were crisp, perfectly responsive, with no or little extraneous comment added, no nuances, an interesting change from what I normally hear. After fifty years of marriage it was difficult to believe that this could be happening to her, but she was serious; she wasn't kidding. I looked at her, waiting for more. She looked back but didn't speak. She waited me out. Her silence meant that it was my turn; ask another question, so I did, feeling a bit like I was the one being interviewed; perhaps I was.

"How is his health?" I asked.

"He appears to be perfectly healthy; he works every day."

"Where?"

"Currently he's working at 'his lady's' house, redoing all of the rooms. He's a master carpenter." She spoke with emphasis, with pride that he is accomplished at his trade.

Quiet again.... 'His lady' I thought to myself, an interesting and kind description of the one who is supplanting her. She spoke with such gentleness of the one who had invaded the nuptial bed.

"Does he have a lawyer, yet?"

"I don't know," she replied.

"What specifically has he done except to tell you that after (I quickly multiplied fifty times 365 on my desk calculator), after 18,250 days or so of being married to you that he now wants out?" Her answer was poignant.

"Well, he doesn't come home any more."

How do divorce lawyers do this every day, I wondered? And why is she here? She surely knows that I'm not a lawyer who practices divorce law. And why is she not pouring out her emotions, not crying, not demeaning him, not speaking in a stream of consciousness in response to my questions, not behaving like others who suffer from their losses, and to whom we can quietly listen, learning from this what we need to know to help them?

So I confronted her. "Why aren't you angry? Why are you calling his girlfriend a lady? Why aren't you crying?"

She read my mind, this bright one. "I have no one waiting in the wings, Mr. Kruse. I won't remarry. I do love my husband." She spoke with such authority, such control, with what appeared to be such unblemished honesty.

"Has his unfaithfulness, his promiscuity, his leaving the marital bed occurred before?"

"I don't think so," she responded. He's certainly never left home — except for the war; he was in the Army."

She didn't react to the bait; the unmasked reference to her husband's adultery was ignored. That subject was not on her agenda. She was as placid as before. Next question.

So we discussed dementia, personality change, considered requesting a mental examination once her husband files divorce proceedings. But she saw no reason to get involved in any of that. "Nothing's wrong with his mind," she said, being both protective of him and serene herself. I did wonder about her, however; how could she remain so objective, and distant and aloof from this new reality in her life. Why isn't she fighting harder?

"Why are you here? What do you want me to do?"

"I don't want a divorce!"

With little armor I'm somehow to stop it. This is a tough assignment, no easy task in a 'no-fault divorce' state. If he wants out of this marriage, fifty years invested in it or not, the court won't stop him. I told her this, something that she already knew, of course. So my job is to prevent it from happening. And I realize that it must be done without injury to him. I'm in a deep sloot.

"If your husband has no lawyer yet, do you think that he would come here to my office with you? All three of us then, can consider what's happening in your lives, and see if there are any solutions, any changes that can be made that will result in a dolce vita?"

She knew the term. "That's what our life has been until now. It has been a sweet life. He may come."

And he did. A few days later in they walked, together; he'd picked her up. She was all dolled up, looking as pretty as before. He had on carpenter clothes — going back to his job at "his lady's" house, I assumed, when he finished here.

I discussed divorce with them, told them how things they acquired during their marriage would be divided, explained what the hearing would be like if they couldn't agree on division of their property and payment of maintenance to which his wife was surely entitled.

I asked them how this event would affect their children and grandchildren, if they would be willing to see a counselor, and even if they'd just not file for a termination of their marriage for awhile, continuing to live apart during this period if that is what he wanted. But he was adamant that he was getting out. I was careful not to argue, just present some alternatives; I even suggested separate maintenance, a condition where they would be legally separated, but still married to each other, but he was disinterested in any suggested alternatives.

"Will you go with me to court," I asked, "and sit in on some divorce hearings, contested ones — so that you can see how ugly and hateful otherwise wonderful people can be when a divorce is occurring. They agreed to that. I checked with the court to determine what was coming up, and I found some doozies — good ones, cases where there'd be lots of anger and shouting and name calling — with aggressive, no-holds barred divorce trial lawyers involved, where the purpose of at least one party, in part, would be to hurt the other, to make the partner pay for this dehiscement in their lives. I could pick such cases by seeing who counsel would be. I know the mean ones — the ones who seem to feel sadistic joy when their adversary's client is feeling pain.

So we went to court — spent almost a full day there, heard juicy parts of a couple such trials.

"See what happens to people who love each other when they come here?" I said during a break. "Is this something that you want to put your wife through? Will you at least let some more time pass before you do this hurtful thing?" All I could really ask for was time; to ask that he not do this yet, to be sure that the lady he has in waiting is worth it, hoping that their amorous relationship would sour, that he would tire of it.

He still liked his wife. I think he still loved her. They sat beside each other during the hearings, walked down the courthouse hall together; had lunch at the same table in the courthouse coffee shop and busily talked to each other; at least they are still friends. I excused myself from the luncheon — some work to do over the lunch hour I told them. I didn't want to intrude in their private conversation in this reunion that might result in the prodigal's return.

But it didn't work. He filed requesting the marriage death. He even hired one of the lawyers he'd seen in action in the divorce court preview that I'd given them.

So I filed a hopeless answer alleging that the objects of the marriage weren't over, but asked for a fair division of the family's small pile of things accumulated over a marriage of fifty years, and I asked for maintenance for her in the event that the divorce was granted.

Her husband had $1,000.00 coming in each month from Social Security and another $800.00 or so from a union carpenter's pension, and earnings from his current carpentry work, whatever that might be.

At the trial he appeared in bib overalls, a carpenter's marking pencil, a one-half inch flat broad point sticking out of his bibs. He had sawdust on his clothes and hair. He'd obviously been working at "his lady's" house, earlier that morning and left for the court hearing at the last minute. He hadn't spruced up for the 10:00 a.m. trial.

He took the witness stand and when it was my turn to examine him, I asked what he was doing with his time and looking up at the judge, he answered, "Like I told Mr. Kruse before, I'm retired."

"Sold your pickup?" I asked.

"No."

"What about your tools? What does a carpenter who's retired do with all his tools?"

"I've got 'em," he said.

"How does a retired carpenter spend his time? What do you do all day?"

"I'm fixin' 'her' house."

"Her?"

"You know — my friend's house."

"You work every day?"

"Yes."

"What time do you start?"

"About 6:00."

"An early riser, huh?"

"Yeah."

"You work until . . . . what time?"

"About 5:00."

"Straight through?"

"I'm tryin' to get this job done!"

That sounded like a yes, but no reason to pursue that. "What are you doing in the house?" I was careful not to say 'her' house — no reason to emphasize the obvious. Besides, 'his lady' was in the audience, watching the trial — easy to spot — not unattractive, younger than her suitor by perhaps twenty years.

"I've gutted it," he said. "It's an old mansion. I'm redoing all the rooms."

"Sounds like a big job."

"It is."

"How soon before you finish?"

"I've got some months to go," he said, explaining the care that he was giving the trim, unlike young carpenters, eager to finish and move on. He was a craftsman. He had lots of pride.

"Getting paid?"

"No."

"Doing this job free?"

"Yes."

"Eight hours a day, five days a week?"

"More than eight — more than five," he answered. His honesty was refreshing. I told him that.

I didn't call my client to testify. It wasn't necessary. We established through her husband's testimony that she received $300.00 a month in Social Security. She was in the home and that was okay with him. She could have it, he said. He'd keep his tools and truck. They didn't have much else. But he didn't want to pay her any alimony. "Can't afford it," he testified. He couldn't care for his new lady with the after-tax and after-alimony income that he would be receiving. He was courting; that's expensive.

The testimony was over. His *mean* lawyer was plenty courteous in this trial, on his good behavior, probably didn't like what was happening any more than I. Besides, I had earlier telephoned his lawyer — asked him where the divorce court was and what I was expected to do. He knew that I wasn't a divorce lawyer and he was being kind.

Time for summation, the carpenter's lawyer urged the judge to deny maintenance, "She can sell the house, Judge; the kids are gone. It's a too big a house for one person, ... " That was the meat of his "no maintenance" theory. Then it was my turn.

"Your Honor, don't require sale of the family home. It's my client's security. If she predeceases her husband he can have the house, but to require it to be sold takes doubly from her. She will have lost both her husband and her home — two priceless jewels lost as she nears entry into her end-life."

"Regarding alimony, your Honor, I suggest to the court that my client's husband hasn't retired from his trade; he's still working. He's simply elected not to be paid, which of course, is injurious to his needs as well as to those of his familial companion of five decades. Your Honor, as long as he has elected to work, attribute value to the task that he is now doing, the master carpenter rate, whatever he agrees that this sum is. I believe that it's $30.00 per hour in this community at this time, but we won't dispute his telling us if that's not accurate. He's been a good and generous husband, and he's an honest man. Multiply that rate times seven hours a day, or six. He shouldn't have to work more than that, and then multiply that by five days a week. How much is that, thirty times seven — $210.00 per day times five — let's round that to a thousand — times four and a half weeks per month, let's call that four — that's $4,000.00 plus $1,800.00 gross from his other sources, his union pension and Social Security, all of course taxable, so subtract the tax; he can tell us how much that is, and from what's left give his wife some maintenance. All these computations are in my client's trial affidavit, and, I believe, are undisputed. Her affidavit shows that she is asking for little and we will leave the determination of her need and her husband's ability to pay to Your Honor."

"NO, I WON'T PAY!"

That loud announcement came from the gallery. It was the carpenter's lady. She was standing. It was as though I had just decreed a duty — as though I were the judge. She'd have no part of my suggestion. There'd be no pay from her to the master builder! She wanted that known. And she shouted that to the judge.

The scene was emotional and unexpected and caught us all off guard except perhaps my client. And for her the outburst was perfectly timed. Out of the courtroom the carpenter's lady went, stomped out, glared at the judge, who up to that point hadn't done a thing against the carpenter's interest. His lady, however, was having a hissy, an hysterical fit, and she wasn't quiet about it. It's a good thing that there was nothing near her to throw. We all would have been targets. The carpenter didn't move, didn't look around, looked straight ahead, wide-eyed, at the judge. He'd only seen his lady's loving side. Now he'd witnessed her anger. He was disbelieving and scared.

"Your Honor," I was still standing, "may I suggest that the court not issue its decree today, that the court hold its order in abeyance until it receives a motion to do otherwise from either counsel?"

"So ordered," the judge said, not even waiting to see what the carpenter's counsel would suggest.

We left. The carpenter and his lawyer had already gone. "What do you make of this?" I asked 'my lady,' my demure client, the bright one.

"It was perfect," she said, as if she knew, as though it were an event that she expected, but did not share with me. For the first time there was some melody in her voice. "He'll be back home now." She spoke with confidence. "He found out what she wanted of him, not him for himself, but for the free work."

"Can you let him come home without scolding, let him be the prodigal and once again affirm your great and patient love of him?"

She looked at me and smiled. It was her affirmation.

I walked her to her car. He was standing beside it. His driver had left, headed back, I suppose to her near-gutted home. My client and her husband embraced, amour propre. They could still have each other. They had some years to go. Their fourscore and ten had not yet been reached. I watched them drive away. Both were crying.

I turned and headed for floor ten, the Holly Sugar Building. It was two more hours before quitting time. I still had work to do.

Love May Be Less Wonderful the Second Time Around

(Medicaid Considerations When Well-to-do, Healthy Clients Remarry And Their Late-in-life Companions Are Less Well-to-do)*

Following the death of near-lifetime companions, spouses with whom our clients have spent a half century or so of their lives, our client-survivors are left to fend for themselves. Now solitary, they sometimes look up "old loves" or meet "new loves" at community senior centers or on alumni trips headed to romantic ports and places.

Well-aged, the perception is that there is little time left and, therefore, wedding plans are sometimes quickly and impulsively made; and breakfast, once again, is arranged on the kitchen table by the one first up on the days which follow the nuptial ritual.

These new couples come to see us for marital agreements; neither wants to be a burden to their late-in-life second spouse. They are joyful, the males often stylish rakes, filled with glee, their grail discovered. Both feel young again and are near giddy.

We may not ask about long-term care insurance when we see them or, if we do, it's not a subject they wish to visit. The conference with these two happy hand-holders is not about sickness and death; it's about life and living. It's about their mutual excitement, their plans together.... It's about loving again.

We get caught up in the merriment, the renewed youth, the energy which accompanies this fresh arrangement, this revisiting of hopeful, carefree, intoxicating, adolescent love — again.

The agreement for which we are scribe voices that neither will have financial responsibility for the other. Their property will be segregated, its income and appreciation singularly benefitting its owner. Contributions will be made in near equal portions for expenses which benefit both. We insert new names into the standard contract — form one in the pre-marital agreement file.

#

The mutual affirmation — I will have no financial responsibility for this love to whom I am to be betrothed — however well-intended by the amorous couple, is read without corresponding joy, and not honored when read by agents of the king — those serving in the government's Medicaid offices. And when the application for public benefit payments is sorrowfully completed by our unknowing and innocent clients following the ambulance ride to the nursing home's emergency vehicle entrance — where the

* This chapter is endnoted. The notes can be found at the end of this chapter.

ill and impecunious spouse is left — our well-to-do, healthy spouses discover that their individually owned resources are added to the assets-available columns within the resources-owned vertical division lines on the appropriate pages of the application for their spouse's Medicaid benefits request. The maximum value in 2000 for resources which the community spouse (whom we represent) may retain is $84,120, (annually indexed to accommodate inflation), in addition to assets that are exempt from consideration, such as a home and car and furnishings.[1]

Our clients are told that for Medicaid benefit purposes, they and their spouses are one — something that the clergyman may have reminded them of when they each pledged their troth to the other. With the voicing of their vows, they became — in the eyes of the king — a single economic unit.

The prenupt, of course, the one which we drafted, will provide that neither spouse is liable for the health care needs of the other — or for his or her needs of any kind — at any time. Any transfer of his funds to her or her funds to him will be strictly voluntary and well-expressed in the agreement. Dutifully, our healthy and rich client has kept her or his income and resources segregated. There's been no commingling, but, of course, that doesn't matter. The healthy spouse learns quickly what "support duty" means, at least in the context of Medicaid, when the second love of her or his life becomes ill.[2]

The wealthy at-home member of this "second-time around" marriage discovers that except for assets which don't count for purposes of Medicaid eligibility — home, car, furniture, miscellaneous minor interests, (such as burial plots and wedding jewelry, and in some states the at-home member's I.R.A. or qualified retirement plan) — all other assets of our now remarried client do. They count! They must be spent before the institutionalized spouse may qualify for Medicaid.[3]

The cash, the stock, mutual funds, E-bonds, long forgotten, secreted in seldom-opened bank safe deposit boxes, the real estate, all carefully protected for the owners in our marital agreements, intended ultimately for our clients' first families, are deemed available to the non-owner spouses. These assets must be used to pay the long-term care centers' monthly costs for services for our clients' ill spouses when their obvious end-life begins until our clients have spent down their long-saved resources to what they and their first families — ultimate beneficiaries — consider to be poverty level residue, and when our wealthy at-home clients, spouses of ill and institutionalized second loves, discover this, their glee is gone.

The bulk of the assets owned by our newly wedded clients all count as though they are in the pockets of the sweats that the loved but institutionalized spouses now wear as they are pushed in Medicare-supplied wheelchairs up and down the hallways of the patients' final home.

The tears in our clients' eyes are both for their now lost second love, and because of the newly discovered reality that they, the healthy spouses, will have to pay the bill — with their own money. Because of our clients' wealth, their spouses' Medicaid applications are denied.

It is not until our clients have denuded themselves of their wealth and possessions to what they feel is near self-impoverishment, roughly a maximum of $82,000[4] in value in 1999, together with state-exempted assets, that Medicaid support — payment for nursing home care — will be available to such persons' spouses.

Except for the very wealthy, which excludes our country's large middle class, however defined, impoverishment comes quickly.

Estate of Knudson[5] tells us that in Idaho, by case law, and presumably in other states as well, when our at-home client dies, his or her assets, those exempt by law during our client's lifetime, principally the house and car and furniture, may be claimed by the state to pay the institutional care costs which Medicaid advanced for the nursing home-boarded spouse of the decedent, depending on when the Medicaid applicant-spouse disposed of her or his assets.[6]

And *Tamler*,[7] a Wisconsin case, advises us that if the at-home spouse dies first, at least in the absence of a binding premarital agreement, the institutionally-housed spouse must elect against our client's Will to take the statutory marital share. If the election is not exercised, such inaction will be treated as though the value of the surviving and ill spouse's rightful share was given away by her or him — resulting in a penalty — loss of Medicaid support for a period equal to what the unclaimed largess would have paid for. For example, if the share not claimed is $60,000 and the average cost of care in the decedent's domicile is $5,000 per month, Medicaid is lost, forfeited for one year. Sixty thousand dollars is divided by the monthly cost of care, and the quotient equals the penalized period, in this example, one year.

Our clients marry in late life at their peril. As spouses of now institutionalized brides or grooms, they are required to pay for the cost of their second spouses' long-term health care expenses. Medicaid considerations require that we investigate long-term care costs in our respective states — around $40,000 a year in Colorado, three times that much in some eastern states. Our clients must expect to contribute that portion of this cost which their now ill and institutionalized spouses are unable to pay.

#

The purchase of long-term care insurance for the newly married and somewhat impecunious spouses of our more wealthy clients may be understood as worthwhile annual dues, payment for the privilege of being married again — a safeguard against costs that may otherwise impoverish our clients who have entered into late-in-life marriages without appreciating the obligations the new relationship may bring.

Alzheimers is a seven to twelve year illness before the patient's mushy brain gives in to death. Multiply that term by the cost of nursing home care in your state to visualize the worst case scenario, the possible cost, the amount of potential erosion of funds saved, intended ultimately and hopefully for first families, our clients' children who are to be the intended recipients of our largess, a form of certificate evidencing the decedents' deserved social immortality.

#

At some point our clients mention the "D" word. The love continues, but this new cost of marriage is injurious — more than the monied mandarin can handle. In-home care at $15.00 per hour,

#

24 hours a day — you do the math.

Our tearful clients testify to us about the love that they have for their mate, and a divorce or sometimes a sham divorce is described to us, a termination of marriage, but not really a severance. Our clients do not want to lose their premarital assets. The love for their new mate may continue, but the cost in money is seen as too great. Ill spouses still able to speak say, in one way or another, from their nursing home bed when divorce is described to them, "Why are you doing this to me? I wouldn't do this to you." Lose one's lifetime savings or experience burdening guilt. This is the dichotomy, the limited range of choice our clients face.

It is about this subject that our clients must be warned. They must be informed of a presence — a shadowy apparition who will attend their wedding ceremonies. The unseen government interest will hear the elders' vows: the promises not only to cherish, but to care in sickness and in health — translate that as "for full costs of care" — at least when sickness overcomes the unmonied one — until death, in fact, does part them, and the public policy responsibility of the spouse for this cost may finally cease.[8]

ENDNOTES

1. *See* 20 C.F.R. § 416.1210 and state regulations relating to exempt assets.
2. *See* State Medicaid Manual, Part 3, Eligibility, Dept. of Health & Human Services, Health Care Financing Administration (Nov. 1994), § 3257, B.3, *Assets*, p. 3-3-109, Transfers of Assets .... "For purposes of this section, assets include all income and resources of the individual [applicant for Medicaid] and of the individual's spouse ...."
3. *See* 20 C.F.R., supra n.1. In Colorado, see Colorado Dept. of Health Care, Policy & Financing Staff Manual, vol. 8, § 8.112.12 F, (eff. 10-10-97). "In computing the value of a couple's resources [those assets not counted] include ... pension funds owned by the non—[Medicaid applicant] spouse (such as IRA's and Keogh Plans), etc. ...." *See also* 20 C.F.R., ch. 111 (4-1-93 edition), § 416.1202, married individual: "In the case of an individual ... who is ... the husband or wife of the [Medicaid applicant], the [spouse's] pension funds are excluded [as available resources to her or his spouse for consideration by Medicaid]. Pension funds are defined as funds held in IRAs ... work related pension plans [and] Keogh plans." *See* 20 C.F.R. §§ 416.1806, 416.1811 and 416.1210. *But see contra, Mistrick v. Div. of Med. Assist.*, 712 A.2d 188 (N.J. 1998).
4. *Supra* n.1.
5. *Estate of Knudson v. Jackman*, (Idaho S. Ct.), No. 23928, 1998, Ida. LEXIS 70, (June 16, 1998), amended 1998 W.L. 762518 (Nov. 2, 1998). The Supreme Court concluded that Idaho may not recover from the estate of a Medicaid recipient's spouse after already recovering from the Medicaid recipient's estate because the asset disposal in this case took place before enactment of a broadened definition of "assets," effective August 10, 1993. *See* discussion in *The ElderLaw Report*, vol. 10, No. 6, (Jan. 1999), p. 5. *See also North Dakota Dept. of Human Services v. Thompson*, (N.D. Sup. Ct., Civil Action No. 980050, 1998 WL 887673 (Dec. 22, 1998), in which the North Dakota Supreme Court ruled that "... federal law permits the recovery of Medicaid expenditures from the estate of the recipient's spouse...." "Keeping Current," *The ElderLaw Rpt.*, vol. 10, No. 8 (March 1999), p. 5. The Report continues "... the definition of 'recipient's estate' contained in federal estate recovery provisions as amended in 1993 'is broad enough to encompass the department's claim against the estate of a deceased spouse of a deceased recipient of medical assistance benefits for the amount of medical assistance paid out, to the extent the recipient at the time of death had any title or interest in assets which were conveyed to his or her spouse (through joint tenancy, tenancy-in-common, survivorship, life estate, living trust, or other arrangement).'" *See also In re Est. of Jobe*, Minn. Ct. App. No. C4-98-1851, 1999 WL 152992 (3-23-99). These cases are discussed in *The ElderLaw Rpt.*, vol. 10, No. 8 (March 1999), p. 5, and vol. 10, No. 11 (June 1999), p. 5.

6. *Id.*
7. *Tannler v. State Dept. of Health and Social Services*, 1196 W.L. 653634, Wisc. Ct. of App., No. 96-0118, (11-12-96).
8. *Estate of Knudson, supra* n.5.

Postscript

"Love May Be Less Wonderful..." is less an essay or story than substantive material designed for lawyers who counsel widowed clients who are contemplating marrying again. In its original form, it was presented as the final section of a lecture given by the author at the Heckerling Institute, The University of Miami School of Law (Jan. 1999). It is a warning to us all, however, if we are contemplating marrying again and our intended is impecunious.

Its message to readers suggests that because the Medicaid program visualizes a husband and wife as a single economic unit, upon remarriage, later in life, the cost of long-term care insurance, paid for by the wealthier spouse on the life of his or her mate, is a reasonable cost for the privilege of being married again. It eliminates the obligation to personally provide economically for the ill and institutionalized second spouse, when costly medical care and long term congregant housing is needed. It makes possible ultimate distribution of accumulated wealth to the elders' first family without erosion caused by being required to pay the cost of the ill second spouse's long-term health care. The inheritance that the wealthier spouse wishes to leave to his or her respective first family is in this way preserved. However unpalatable, termination of marriage may be the only other alternative to avoid the high cost of long-term care required by the ill and institutionalized second spouse when her funds or his are insufficient.

Divorce and the anguish it creates for older married couples is the topic of the prior essay (Chapter 24). Elder lawyers preserve, if possible, the marriage status and search for ways to avoid an unwanted severance of the couple's commitment to each other. "Love May Be Less Wonderful..." suggests that the foresightful purchase of long—term care insurance may resolve the economic dependence one spouse may unintentionally force upon the other, caused by the rule (where Medicaid is requested) that married couples will be treated as a single economic unit. The funds of both are deemed available for the long-term support needed by the one who is now institutionalized. Without this pressure love may still be wonderful, and the couple's care, companionship and commitment to each other can continue.

PART NINE

"We Sell Cookies, Too"

The evening meal, first setting, begins promptly at 5:00. A few minutes before 4:00, I arrived at the assisted living center and signed the guest book, the home's requirement if you're a stranger, one not living there. Such persons, including me, have to check in and out, even though I'm a regular stranger, seeing various residents who occupy the large four-story 200-unit building, several times a month.

Already, small clusters of the home's occupants have begun to gather, some sitting in the building's large great room, one filled with overstuffed furnishings and strong straight chairs as well, the latter used by those with bad backs and those whose flaccid muscles make it difficult for them to extricate themselves from the softer models.

Those waiting on dinner are carping that, "It still isn't open," even though dinner's "only an hour away," but a large chair has been placed in front of the dining room entrance, and to all who live there, its message is clear — stay out!

This scene occurs nightly; it's always the same, but not giving up hope, one day at 4:00 p.m. the chair may not be there, and the early arrivals will get in and seize their favorite dining spots.

#

The groups, keeping one eye on the dining entrance, keep the other on me. They remind me of tropical fish whose bulging eyes are separately controlled, each eye looking in a different direction. Those in waiting here, anxious not to miss a thing, seem to have developed that capacity, too. They knew I was coming, and even knew whom I would be seeing that afternoon. I "high-fived" a couple of spirited males. One first pretended that his hand was a .38 and his index finger, a pretend gun barrel. He jokingly aimed it at me, "ka-pow" he half-grunted. "I'm hit," I said in mock anguish. His buddies laughed.

A couple of ladies came up for hugs, and a group sitting in the overstuffeds called out for me to "come on over; sit a spell." They were retired farm people. The guys all had on Allis Chalmers caps. They looked new, evidence that they've never been worn by one currently tilling fields. The men still wore bib-overalls, cleaner and bluer than those they had worked in all of their lives, but "bibs" remain their uniform. It reminds others of their importance. They spent their lives farming and they're proud of that. I could imagine them in Western Kansas, sitting in the town's "spit-and-cuss" club, playing cards, waiting for the wheat to grow tall enough to harvest, toothpicks between their lips, to be replaced by wheat shafts, come cutting time. They had the pre-meal toothpicks in place now, barely an inch or so peeking out of the corner of lips still looking to a man a bit sunburned, evidence of working outdoors in sun country with no sunblock or similar protection.

Still not 4:00. I've learned not to be early, not even by a moment. The client won't be ready and the opening minutes will be spent listening to apologies about how awful — what appears to me to be a pretty spotless front room — looks. "I just didn't have time to get to it," a hint that I came too soon. I looked at the bulletin board. A typed document held by six thumbtacks (making it harder to remove) listed the week's activities. Tuesday through Friday the beauty and barber salon is open. Today is Thursday, and not much is happening. Joe Westgate led a Bible study at 10:00. A resident bus left at 1:00 and again at 3:00 for the grocery, a daily event. This evening a piano player is coming to play, "your old favorites." Presumably, those attending in the room with the overstuffeds can sing along. Saturday through Monday the beauty salon is closed, working only Tuesday through Friday is heavy duty, I thought, for a building of 200 rooms, but perhaps some didn't get themselves made up every week — not much to trim anyway, on most of the men.

I moseyed down the nearest corridor looking for Suite 129,

"...right side, half-way down." Those were my instructions. I found it. Some pretty silk flowers filled a straw basket tacked to a door. A small brass plate identified Mr. & Mrs. — , the occupants. I knocked. It was precisely 4:00.

It took nearly a minute before the door opened; there is a last-minute check-out going on, I imagined, to be sure that everything is in order for the new guest, but still there will be apologies that everything is not picture-perfect.

"Where's Mikki?" the director at a Colorado Springs senior care organization, the pretty resident asked as I introduced myself, and started to enter. She looked down the long hallway. "She's to be here." Mikki is the Executive Director of Silver Key Senior Services, one heavily relied on by many elders in this community.

The 95-year-old resident had prepared for this meeting. Her hair had been done that day, it appeared, nothing out of place. The staff in the beauty salon this Thursday were pros. Her hair was a pretty light-colored gray. She had soft colored gloss brushed on her lips and a rosy glow in her cheeks. She had on slacks that matched the color of her hair accented by a gold necklace, bracelet, and attractive pin, a sunburst, small, about the size of a quarter on a pretty rose-colored knitted blouse. She was a good dresser, classy. Her mind, I discovered, was acute as well, as soon as she got over Mikki's being tardy. "Where's Mikki?" she kept asking for the first twenty minutes of our meeting. Good question, but I didn't know. My suggestion that we telephone her was vetoed, so we continued our small talk, social chatter. She needed to become comfortable in the presence of this stranger.

Her tall, handsome and quiet husband sat on a straight chair on my left, a foot or so in front of me, facing his wife so I could see his profile when he wasn't looking straight at me. His hair was perfectly combed, sprayed, to be held in place. His mustache, now gray, looked like Clark Gable's, so did he, otherwise. Like the actor, he looked dashing. I wondered if he'd ever been a model.

He could be one now, if he had the energy, although, at 92, three years younger than his wife, his body was showing its age. He was thin, too thin, skeletal. The members of the overstuffed crowd who were waiting in the great room ready for their supper, like-new billed farm caps pulled into place, ready to shield them from any ray of sun that might slip through the solid roof, told me that the guy I was to see *has* been ill. "Is" might be a more accurate verb.

"It's too high here," my male friend spoke, actually half shouted, "7500 feet! I've got to get to lower ground. We're moving, going to Pike's Manor, lower [altitude]," he motioned downward. Actually, Pike's is a horizontal move, about three miles away, still in the shadow of Pikes Peak, Colorado's 14,000 foot high mountain, and no less nearer the clouds than where he's living now, but in his mind, the new location, still in Colorado Springs, is lower and so breathing will be easier.

The couple, at 95 and 92, are childless; they have no relatives that they could name; their collaterals are "probably dead now," the couple said, or if not, might as well be. There is no contact between these relative-strangers if any are alive and the couple in Suite 129. There is no other city with heavier air where they would have comfort going, no family who could look in on them. "Yeah, lower," I said, acknowledging that the move already decided on, was a good idea.

"What was your work when you were younger," I asked the Mr.,

a name given to her husband when "the Mrs." spoke about him as we talked. "Same as you," he slowly replied. "I was a salesman." Coming from him, I was amused, perhaps it was a compliment, better than being a lawyer.

"What did you sell?" I inquired.

"Cookies," he replied.

I let a moment pass. I loved the metaphor.... "So do I," I quietly replied.

Thirty minutes had passed. It was apparent that Mikki wasn't coming. "Why don't we start," I suggested. "Why am I here? What is it that I might be able to help you with?"

"Our wills," the Mrs. said. "We want to redo them. Can you do that?"

"Perhaps," I said. That's a large part of what I do every day — 35 to 40 plans a month, typically, but they don't need to know that — better to see what they have in mind first, and I needed background.

"Tell me about your family," I suggested. They do. There is none. A couple of first cousins once removed, persons really unknown to them, no relationship, an occasional card at Christmas from someone "we don't know" but who might be a relative "way down the line." But there is no person close in consanguinity to them. We'll have to publish to unknown heirs when the last of these two die. There's no way to know unless, come next Christmas, a card is received with a return address, hopefully saved, so we'll have a lead. The couple promised that, beginning now, they'll save all the cards and personal mail along with the envelopes in which the messages arrive.

So much for relatives. No children; none deceased; no issue; no prior marriages; no births out of wedlock; no known ancestors — and no remaining friends. "They all died," they repeated together. There's no need for these two to have a one-bedroom home in tourist country to avoid putting up with the Winnebago® crowd, those who call when they arrive and expect the hapless home-town relatives to feed and entertain them while they're here with the oversized sleeper van parked, unused on the front street for the duration, using their relative's digs and car.

I looked at the couple's existing wills taken from a hide-away in the bedroom and handed to me. Done on long, legal scratch, pica-size letters, ten to an inch, all the capitalized "to wits" the drafter could squeeze in, and done on faded, water-marked bond, Crane, not inexpensive parchment, and old. The Mr. and Mrs. had been married to each other for more than 70 years and the wills appeared to have been created about that long ago.

"Who are these people?" I asked reading from the fading pages. They were relatives, long ago dead. Not a name on the Crane who was still living and none had heirs known to this couple.

"Okay. What's the new will to say? Who's to benefit?"

"Children," the Mr. said.

"And Silver Key," his wife added, Mikki's charity, the Colorado Springs agency that looks after our elder population.

"What children?"

"The burned ones."

"Shriner's Hospital?" I asked.

"Yeah, that's the one."

"Half each?"

"Yes." They both agreed.

"What do you two own? What will these two charities be receiving?"

A small box was produced, 10 by 12, four inches deep, steel, aged-looking, but no rust, no lock or hinges. It had been hidden in the bedroom (the room any thief first searches). I pried its lid open. It was difficult. This home "safe" hadn't been opened in a while.

I began taking out its contents, item by item — a teaching certificate, "Temporary Credentials," it read. It entitled its holder to instruct in the state's high schools. On thick bond, it was yellowed, and it was difficult to read the fading signatures. The creases where the thick document resembling parchment had been folded were now dark, striped vertically across the memento once important to its owner and obviously still valued; it was in the box, on top, the first treasure I was allowed to discover.

"Miss it?" I asked.

"What?"

"Miss teaching?"

"No. I made $130 a month though," she said, "enough to buy my first fur coat. I taught just a few years."

Beneath the prized certificate credentialing the Mrs. in 1927 in a profession that I think she does miss, were gold, plastic CD holders, near legal envelope size, cracked from age, held together with a single thin, red band, holding the one-inch accumulation together. They were empty, all of them.

"Where are the CDs?" I asked.

"In the bank vault," the Mr. said, as though I might think them stupid not to have the certificates there. Saved were their aged containers because they may be useful some day. When the CDs are due, they'll be turned in without their plastic carriers. Those are salvaged, held in the small, portable "safe" at home — the box I was privileged to enter.

Deeper in the box was the Mr.'s Salesman of the Year award given to him by the John H. Quaker Company, makers of "fine cookies." The award emphasized the product, but the Mr.'s name had been typed in, pica size again, and it was authentic, bore a seal, and the president's stamped signature, and had a tri-colored border. I wondered how many cookies he'd pedaled to get this honor. "Girl Scout of the Year," came to mind, but I bit my tongue, positive that he wouldn't appreciate the analogy.

"Good job! Why isn't this on the wall?" I inquired.

He didn't answer; dumb question.

It's a privilege that we have as lawyers, being invited by our clients to see their possessions, what they've saved, memories that are important to them. It takes awhile to get through even a small box. We listen to the stories that each piece of scratch invites. The important stuff is in the box. This couple listed their CDs and their value, the stock they've hoarded, lists of various accounts in sundry banks in the city, all in joint tenancy. The real stuff is in the vault, but in their box were their lists, carefully drawn, but with old lists not discarded, none dated. I supposed that the list nearest the top of the pile was the most recent but there is no way of knowing. The lists are all similar but the bank names and the amounts changed. When accounts became due they shopped for the best rates, I imagined.

"I need to go to the bank," the Mrs. said. "I need more money in the [checking] account." "Check account," she called it. "I'll take some out of savings." She could do that. If her lists are accurate, there is plenty there. She intended to deposit another $10,000.00 in the account that could be drawn on with checks, "for emergencies," she said.

"How much is in your check-account now?" I asked, but the Mrs. wasn't sure that I needed to know that, so she said she didn't know. But she's a bright one. I know she did, I'd bet, to the penny. The other accounts totaled several hundred thousand dollars if the lists are near accurate. She didn't want me to be critical because she had too much already in the low-interest "emergency" account, not untypical of monied elders.

Judging by the size of this family's wealth, the "Cookie Salesman of the Year Award," should have been framed, and there had to be more than one. "Salesman, same as you," was obviously a good one. He could teach us all a bit about selling, and I suspect, much about saving a large part of what we earn, as well.

The chimes on the wall clock played their evening melody — six bongs. I'd been there two hours, time now to leave. This couple has the second seating in the dining room down the corridor. I didn't want them to miss that. There will be curious residents at their table wanting to know all about the long visit which they had with their lawyer. We said our goodbyes. The Mrs. gave me a hug, like I imagined she had done for not a few of her students in her short, Depression-era teaching tenure; I saluted the Mr. and he, me.

Once again, I had been invited into the private world of an older couple who are living in their end-life, still managing to stay together, energized by each other's strength, physical ailments aside, updating their plan of wealth transmission, answering personal questions about what they owned and what their stuff is worth, tolerating the lawyer's quizzing and prying respectfully. I was careful to compliment them on their successes, their awards and their significant cash accounts. The community views lawyers as wealthy and clients fear that their savings will be seen as a pittance in comparison, not worth the lawyer's time to plan. They're often embarrassed that they don't have more, seeing wealth acquisition as evidence of success, an area in which they sense they've failed. And so, the lawyer affirms that they have done well, careful not to demean what is sometimes frighteningly small savings with which some must face their future.

We sell cookies, too, sweet biscuits to our clients, treats that make them feel better, assurance that the plans that they have for transmission of their wealth, however large or small, will be possible and will make the lives that follow theirs better than those lives would otherwise be.

The purpose for this couple's lifetime savings safely stored in accounts in banks all over their city is now crystallized, or nearly so. Burned children will be better, perhaps healed, because the Mr. is making this possible. And other elders, more needful than their aged benefactors, will have more enriched lives. The Mrs. is making this happen.

Tonight this couple began their evening meal with dessert, sweet cookies that sated their appetites. They are filled now with peace of mind, assurance that their assets, saved over nearly a century will pass to their "children," two fine charities. This couple will share their treasures collected and identified in their box. They will be remembered as people who made a difference, providing needed benefits to others which would not have happened except for them.

Their plan is simple, division of what they leave behind between two caring charities. Mikki, forgiven for not arriving on this evening, a trusted friend, is the one who will see that this plan is followed.

"What will happen [to our assets] when we're both gone, [to all that's been saved, salvaged from a disciplined life?"], a bothersome question to this couple in their ninetieth years, now resolved. As I leave, they head down the long and narrow corridor, walking slowly arm in arm towards the dining hall. No more dessert for them tonight, though; they've had their fill, furnished in part by their "salesman — same as you." ...We sell cookies, too.

*Remembering Alice**

She was 78 when I first met her, a native of the county that extends beyond West Colorado Springs where the State Capitol was once home, beyond several mountain towns ending near the city limits of Woodland Park. The next stop after that is Cripple Creek, famous for its historic gold mines and Bennett Street bordellos. Eastward, the county contains spots by the highway housing the adventurous in Midwestern America, small places, towns colorfully known as Ellicott, Yoder, Peyton and Rush. You'll miss them if you're driving on Highway 94, a two-lane vein, and happen to blink. Alice Backus seldom left this county. It was her lifetime home, and for all she cared it could have been Paris or New York City. She was a lady. She would have fitted in anywhere. Alice Backus was "Mrs. Backus," to her friends. No one in her presence referred to her as Alice, following her marriage, although all of her friends were known to her by their first names. She had the regal bearing that made such an arrangement just natural.

At age 78, Mrs. Backus was still an active member of the Colorado Springs Dental Auxiliary. It provided an important social outing for her. Her colleagues in this special sorority were or had been married to doctors of dentistry, men of position. They were, therefore, women of status, on high pedestal, socially important, at least by mid-twentieth century standards in El Paso County, Colorado.

She loved the auxiliary. Few outsiders were admitted even as guests to this privy council. On one occasion, however, my wife, Carolyn, was, and she, as far as I know, was the only lawyer's wife permitted entry. It was there that she met this grande dame, and it was shortly thereafter that I became the lawyer for Mrs. Backus.

Growing up on the West Side, the city's path one took to get to the early mining towns including Cripple Creek, Alice Backus took stock of what went on along the streets of the West Side. Miss Laura Belle, a prominent West Side madame (eventually, The Madame for Laura Belle's, a well-known house of great repute, entertainment for Cripple Creek's hard rock miners), paraded up and down the West Side's cobbled avenues dressed to the nines, regardless of the time of day, made up "real proper," hair coiffured in a French roll or dramatic pompadour. She had beautiful hair, Alice remembered, always accompanied by a hat placed at a just-right angle. Her accouterments included an emerald-colored street-length fancy dress and a lacy, never-opened bumbershoot, except when the sun shone in a cloudless sky. It was part of her costume.

Miss Laura Belle was an elegant sight, patrolling her territory, charming, courteous — and generous. She was lavishly charitable. The hard rock miners made that possible,

* This chapter is endnoted. The notes can be found at the end of this chapter.

and if someone needed an offering Miss Belle's purse would be shared.

As a young girl, growing up on the Western edge of the Springs, Alice was not allowed, ever, to look at the West Side's most prominent member. Her mother made sure that her daughter was aware of the incarnate evil that Laura Belle represented. To acknowledge her presence, let alone emulate her, either in dress or manner, however stylish, was unthinkable. She was evidence of Satan at work, his persuasive hoopoe[1]. Alice, of course, peeked whenever Miss Belle was sighted and presumably when Alice was unaccompanied by her mother. She loved her pretentious outfits, her frilly hats and bumbershoots and she was captivated by her regal bearing, a quality that Mrs. Backus adopted, consciously or not, as an important part of her own *persona*.

In mid-life Alice met and married a Colorado Springs dentist — not a West Sider, but a resident of Colorado Springs North End, the preferred acreage for mine owners who got rich quick in the rush for Cripple Creek gold. They built homes, large mansions in the city's North End. Dr. Backus didn't own a large, grand house, but rather a small cottage, situated on a North End side street, close enough to the homes of the high rollers, however, to be a coveted North End homeowner, and to give his regal lady social status in this still small but emerging mid-western city.

She filled his home with books. She loved to read, evidence perhaps of the lively imagination that accompanied her adolescence. She studied words and their origins and purchased the entire set of *Modern Eloquence* — in ten volumes, handsomely bound, sent to her by the John D. Morris Company, Philadelphia, Pennsylvania. She still had the set in a place of honor on her bookshelves the day that she died.

Alice Backus loved radio preaching, the kind you reach by dialing to the far sides of the half-circles containing the frequency settings on the old hand-turned radio dials in the days before scan-buttons and station-memory keys became the only choice. A station in Del Rio, Texas, late most evenings had just enough megahertz to be heard in North Colorado Springs and Alice could pick it up with only modest static on her old upright floor model RCA. She twisted and turned the dials until she got it tuned in just right.

She sent for the cheaply made Bibles the preachers hawked, printed on thin paper filled with acid, making the largely unread books self-destructing after a few hot summers in the attics where such things are eventually stored — for use by others some day. Alice had lots of Bibles, all sizes and colors, some put together with likenesses of the radio preachers that brought their Hell-and-Brimstone tirades nightly to good people such as Alice who wanted to become even better. She listened to them, as she had to her mother, to find out how. She had boxes of pledge envelopes and prayer cloths that were somehow to be draped over the radio during the broadcasts, not thick enough, unfortunately, to fully muffle the speaker. Most of those that I saw that had been sent to Alice, looked something like a mass-produced cheap cotton Woolworth hanky. I never asked how they worked, or even if they ever did work, or even if she ever even used them. There was no reason for me to discuss theological or metaphysical taste with her. She seldom mentioned it anyway. I suspect that listening to the damnation of evil wouldn't harm her and it passed the time, evidencing good intention on her part to please the Lord. Listening to the Del Rio, Texas airwaves, if nothing else, brought some noise to her isolation after Dr. Backus's death and reduced the unwanted sound of her own solitude.

Mrs. Backus wrote several wills over the two decades or so that I knew her. The character of the devisees never changed, only their names. There appeared to be a limited life to the Del Rio, Texas-based preachers.[2] One would pass from the scene and another would follow and take his place. The message, however, judging from the literature stacked in her home seemed to be the same — some assurances that God loved her, followed by requests for money so that undefined good works could continue in the Omniscient one's struggle with the Devil. Evangelical bi-polar fundamentalism was the belief-speak of the tabloids and pamphlets regularly streaming into her home: God and the Devil were locked in immortal combat and God needed the foot soldiers' money, which without rational explanation, was the method by which the Devil would ultimately be undone, God emerging as the victor.

Periodically, Alice would call me to change her will. I dutifully did that each time she called. She never sought my approval for her bequests; I never offered my opinion. As far as I could tell, every will she'd written, at least those following Dr. Backus's death, were structured the same. The whole of the estate was to pass to her "religious" charities.

In her mid-90's Mrs. Backus was delivered by the North End hospital — "The" Hospital in Colorado Springs — at least for North Enders who coveted private, not municipal, hospital care — to her final home. It was the private pay section of Springs Village. It wasn't a village, of course; it was a tri-level nursing complex looking like and smelling of an antiseptic odor which permeates all institutional end-life places. Private pay had the top floor, though, and those with rooms on the west side, a view of the Rockies.

Her Dental Auxiliary friends visited Mrs. B regularly, including my wife, who had been drummed into the corp — an honorary dentist's wife. My profession was ignored, a necessity in order to get this new member in. Few of those who attended the periodic meetings had live husbands around anymore, anyway, so perhaps credentialing no longer mattered.

Faithfully, my wife visited her elder friend. Mrs. Backus had a demeaning "Alice," room sign on the door to her new quarters. My wife tried in vain to have the crayoned cardboard sign remade. She asked the staff to respect the request to call Alice by the name she loved — Mrs. Backus — but they didn't. Their promises otherwise were made with fingers crossed.

Twice a month or so, Carolyn would stop by at noon bringing her friend a MacDonald's fish sandwich. They would split it. It's accompaniment was Dry Sack Sherry, Alice's contribution to the meal, one small glass each. I'm told that the combination, particularly because of the tartar sauce that accompanied the fish, tasted as horrid as it sounds. Whenever Mrs. Backus would be asked if she were running low of the noon time booze, she always "feared" that she was. A new bottle "would be nice." Carolyn dutifully produced another. When Alice Backus died and the bank-executor cleaned out her room, I was called by them to pick up the mountainous cache of her unopened horde, secreted beneath clothing on her closet floor, reserved for the day, perhaps, when Carolyn might not come. It was Alice's contingent plan, I imagine.

Alice Backus had her beloved radio in her room and could still work the dial and to the day of her death still listened to the Del Rio preachers. She played the set quietly. No one complained. But this resulted in more will changes. New preachers were heard from, replacement officers in the celestial brigade. More money was needed. The battle was no mere skirmish, and not over. "Change the names," summarized her command to me.

Two weeks before our friend died, she called me — a will change I surmised. I headed to Springs Village.

"Am I doing the right thing?" she wanted to know.

"Right thing?"

"Should I give my money to the churches?"

By that, of course, she meant the radio preachers — those who had entertained and sustained her over many years, perhaps sixty or so — different names — same sermon.

Reverse Mortmain went through my mind. Rather than giving to ecclesiastical interests just before death, she would be taking away.

I hesitated. I bit my tongue.

"Who would the new beneficiaries be?" I asked. There was no reply.

"Do you think that you're doing the wrong thing? Your Will leaves your estate, in part to your church, and most of what you have to your radio programs. What do you want changed?"

"Nothing," she replied. "But you've never told me how you felt about what I'm doing."

"Mrs. B, you don't need by approval, do you? Hasn't your plan always been to leave your money the way you've done it? Who else is there that you want included?"

"I want to know if I'm doing the right thing."

Her Will is certainly offensive to my personal values, and I thought that the campaign between the Devil and God ended long ago, or should have, destined to the metaphysical archives, like the once hot topic, "How many angels can dance on the head of a pin?"[3]

"Right thing!" What does that mean? Who defines what is morally correct? Is this an unverbalized responsibility of the will drafter? Am I charged in this case with destroying my client's sixty or seventy-year long estate plan by my definition of acceptable beneficiaries, by my notion of what is right or even useful? Should I list my charities, describe the thievery to which Mrs. Backus has unwittingly contributed for most of her adult life for whatever reason? May I do that?

Should I tell an educated, competent, dying woman, retired school teacher, client and friend, that she has been relying on a mythology espoused by those I consider ill-informed at best, thieves, at worst, using their audiences' collective fear of infinite questions — ones we have no capacity to fathom — to benefit themselves?

Can human beings comprehend the infinite issues — who created God? If space is not infinite, then what's on the other side of it? To the Del Rio preachers, these metaphysical mysteries are knowable. Their faith, assuming sincerity, is presented as truth, not hopeful speculation. Is this my responsibility, to redirect her wealth in the last throes of her life to interests that I believe are more honorable than hers?

I held her hand and kissed it. I did that often, "classy," she called it, European — French, she believed. I smiled at her.

"Am I doing the right thing?" she insisted.

Our roles were now reversed. No longer scrivener, I'm now parent consoling child. I looked into her eyes. I spoke her first name in her presence for the first time. "Alice, you're doing the right thing."

She was relieved. Her demeanor softened. She smiled for the first time since I entered the room. Confirmation, that was what she wanted. Not a change of plan — not my charities, not my sense of what is right, not metaphysics, not theology, but support, validation, assurance from a trusted friend.

Two weeks later I received the early morning call. "Mrs. Backus died during the night," the attendant said. I knew it was a peaceful passing.

ENDNOTES

1. A salmon-pink bird with black and white wings and tail, large erectile crest, and long decurved (bent down) bill, a supposedly stupid appearance. See synonym, dupe, *The Oxford Encyclopedic English Dictionary, Third Edition*, (Oxford University Press, New York, 1996), p. 437, and hoopoe, p. 680).
2. An interesting article on one of the Del Rio preachers appears in *The New Yorker*. *See* "Miracle Man," (American Memories), *The New Yorker*, April 12, 1999, p. 64, arguably "America's most flamboyant radio faith healer," the Pentecostalist J. Charles Jessup.
3. This early theological debate had two answers: All angels, because those supporting this theory believed that angels were incorporeal, didn't occupy space nor have weight, and therefore, all angels could dance on a pinhead; others believed that angels were corporeal, occupied space and had weight, therefore, no such being could fit on a pinhead. This was a big time argument among early metaphysicists.

Trusting Mikki

"Mikki said you'd help me?", a somewhat stooped gentleman, his graying hair trimmed in an economical crew, announced. His statement was phrased as a question. He wasn't sure that he'd received the "straight skinney" from Mikki Kraushaar, the guardian angel who daily puts herself on the line protecting the Colorado Springs community's frail and aging population from their stressful fears.

My 4:00 o'clock appointment, an older man, was accompanied by what appeared to be an even older elder woman, whom I silently assumed was his mother. Tall, her flowing white hair fell fully over her shoulders, and almost hid a pretty ribbon. Her cheeks were hollow, her nose prominent. Toothless perhaps, her thin lips were turned downward, a physical frown that appeared permanent, her body's and mind's acknowledgment of a hard life and long-term anguish.

"We — my wife and I — went to a free seminar," he explained. It was then that I realized that it wasn't son talking. It was husband, accompanied by his wife. But she looked so much older, her large bone structure belying her frailty, her physical and mental weariness accentuating age.

"When we go to a nursing home, we were told, our life expectancy there will be four years. That'll wipe us out!" He spoke as though the unwanted event was a *fait accompli*.

Was the seminar-merchant selling four-year nursing home insurance, I silently wondered? Actual life expectancy in such care centers is less than two years, around 20 months. Perhaps this was a come-on by a trust-merchant. Later, in a private "free" 30 minute session, a revocable trust might be suggested as The Answer — the way to avoid loss of even exempt property. It's a common enticement, preying on the anxiety of the elder community, using exaggeration and lies for self-gain.

My contemplation was interrupted.

"We've decided to give our stuff to our kids." The announcement was almost blurted out, his words almost staccato.

"How many children do you have," I asked?

"Five left. Can we do that?" The message was clear: don't change the subject. Answer the question. He looked at me with his inch-long unlimp crew-cut hair shooting erect from every follicle. His eyes were intense. One way or the other, he was asking, are we going to lose our home, all of our stuff, the substance of our memories, things pack—ratted away that give our lives meaning. Will all this be taken? Not wanting to lose all they had worked for, giving it to the kids was imagined as the better of two poor choices.

I looked at his wife, the quiet one. She was younger by three years than her 75-year old husband, spokesman for them both in this feared adventure — talking to a lawyer in a tenth-floor law office — trusting Mikki. Because of age they risked losing everything. That's what she learned from the free seminar — but she could handle this, too.

She had borne more than five children and experienced a life of significant poverty and deprivation, lived on meager income, worn out now from her catch-as-catch-can living, nurturing and rearing five babies into adulthood and losing at least one, blunting disappointment by expecting the worst.

"What are you talking about giving away? What do you two own?"

The stoic couple owned their home. An $8,500.00 mortgage yet to be paid caused them to think of the bank as owner; they drove an old car, and had little else. One daughter lived in a home beside theirs which they were buying, their sole investment. The assessor valued it at $35,000.00, but its $18,000.00 mortgage and $350.00 monthly payments including utilities, made it a near liability. The daughter paid them rent of $400.00 a month. It was like a growth stock for them, a long-term investment that eventually — an undefined point in time — would result in something good for them.

Social Security brought in $710.00 a month to husband, $300.00 to wife; the rental was break-even, adding nothing, a liability when something needed fixing. But it gave them hope. It could someday, somehow, be worth something.

Should they be told to gift it now, let one child, or all children own it? The modest gift would not be injurious — five months of Medicaid ineligibility at worst, and could be arranged before year end.

They were told about Kennedy-Kassebaum, the federal law criminalizing the gratuitous transfer of one's assets in order to qualify for publically supported long-term care, and the Medicaid ineligibility period and a transfer that could be made by one of them to the other, and a power of attorney for gifting their assets which could insure this result. But they were also told, "You don't have to give your things away, nothing. You're just fine as you are."

This message was that their lives didn't have to be disrupted, not yet, and with some luck, perhaps never. After all, that was the unspoken question that they had asked their lawyer that day — "Are we going to lose the comfort that we enjoy, the security in knowing that what we have is ours," earned by mutual effort during a life together, however ungenerous the repayment for their contributions to Life had been.

The questions our clients ask us are sometimes misphrased. They ask us what for them is safe for us to hear — not what they really want to know.

Some years ago, an attractive young physician's wife made an appointment with her lawyer "about my husband," she said. "He's been unfaithful," she cried. "I can't live with that."

"Sure," an inexperienced young attorney replied. "Adultery — that's a good ground (for divorce). With that we can probably get you some good alimony, too."

But, of course, that wasn't her question, was it? She hadn't asked for, (or even about) a divorce. She didn't ask for anything — except a listening ear.

#

"What has he done?" might have been a good reply. What is it that she couldn't live with? Perhaps it was her own infidelity, her reaction to his breach of trust. It was this, I ultimately learned, after pleadings had been filed, which was the fundament of her grief. She couldn't live with the flaw she discovered in her own character. "I've been unfaithful," was too hard for her to phrase.

Medicaid qualification may, similarly, not be the real subject of the law office appointment. It might be the interested children's purpose, as they accompany their nearest ancestor to the law office, "to protect him or her," from the lawyer with whom they are not familiar. But the elders themselves may be unmotivated to follow their children's planning suggestions, so they've been brought to the lawyer to have these solutions confirmed. Indeed, their real question might be — whether or not we can protect them from their acquisitive children — difficult to ask directly, when the children are needful and their help seen as so very necessary. But it's not comfortable for our elder clients to question the motives of those they bore and nurtured and who now, as the parents have aged and are somewhat frail, appear to be so caring. So an heroic and stoic posture by the elder client is assumed. The government is the enemy — Congress the villain — and the stated purpose of the appointment is mechanical; "What can I do to get Medicaid — if some time I have to go to a nursing home?" A salivating child may or may not be present to hear the answer.

#

Before we answer the question that it phrased, however, if it's ever answered, we need to discover the question that is not asked by our clients: "Must I do this? Must I lose all that I've worked for — all of my things — before I die? Must my exit from this life be without status, evidenced by what I leave behind?"

We identify with our property. We're proud of it. This feeling intensifies when we are threatened with its loss. We see this in divorce, and we witness it as our clients age as tangible property memorandums are made out listing the "heirlooms" that form their collections, careful about whom they may let receive it. As members of the human family, our status and social position are reflected at least in our own minds by what we own. Where we live similarly encourages our sense of self—importance. Is it a surprise that the root word for status is estate?

In Latin we learn that our status is the estate that we have in property. Transferring that wealth, however meager, is a psychological loss, a giving up of our physical evidence of importance. In this loss we have lessened our stature, our importance in the community. In the nursing home Medicaid wing we are suddenly expendable, sacrificed, involuntarily discommitted from community importance, without estate, without status, without stature.

There are reasons beyond physical frailty that result in life in a nursing home being short-lived, that cause appetites to cease, interest in life outside the asylum to lessen, and the solitude of death to become the subject of the inmates' fantasies.

Denuded of wealth, however modest by meaningless spend down or gift, placed in sanctuary, with little or nothing save physical life itself to live for, medicated for restraint and depression, is it any wonder that the questions that the elder client introduces to us for answer are restrained? "Can we qualify for Medicaid?" may be the question that is asked. Whether our clients really want to qualify for this end-life gratuity or not, may not be asked, and if answered, may not be answered truthfully.

#

"... nor cares [the] fly about gilded ceilings."*

#

The couple seemed suddenly cheerful. They love their kids and I would bet that their five children love them, too. But a greater good must be served than the salvaging of property — dignity, pride, and self-worth, for example. A sense of status, of personal accomplishment is witnessed in a couple's feelings about their small frame dwelling and its next door companion, a tiny rental, certainly far distant from the city's Park Place® and Boardwalk®. Both dwellings are probably in need of paint, but they are clean homes, I imagine, sparkling clean, if I read right the role of my client with the flowing white hair and pretty ribbon. Her self-worth and pride come from playing the role she defined for herself well. She is the mother of five good children, one, unsurprisingly, a daughter in her second year of pediatric residency, and she knows that. And she doesn't want her relationship with them to change. She's still mom, still quietly in charge — a person of status. It will stay that way until she dies, and thereafter it will be a comfort to her children as they contemplate the great gifts that their parents imparted to them, verbalized in the children's lifetime memories.

Holding his wife's hand, he put his other arm around her thin body. There was a tender squeeze. "We can keep the home, Honey — and the rental if we want." They cried. So did I.

* Horace, Od., ii, 16, 9, quoted by Michel de Montaigne, "Of the Inequality Amongst Us," *Selected Essays*, N.Y., Dover Press, NY (1966), pp. 29, 32; "[the]" replaces Horace's translator's term "that."

*Ellen**

"Sorry I'm late," a near-bald 70-year-old businessman said. "Me, too," I thought. He was scheduled for an hour, my first appointment of the day. I'll be off schedule now by 45 minutes, apologizing to all the clients that follow.

Of course, he'll have a reason for his tardiness, they all do, but not necessarily the ones they give. First time clients, not knowing what to expect, unsure that the lawyer they've selected can be trusted, fearing that the attorney will be judgmental and won't understand them are among the reasons. But there's almost always initial discomfort and it sometimes translates into not being punctual. Occasionally the new client even brings a friend, a companion who "drove me here, [so] is it all right if she comes in with me?" There is safety in numbers, and with a friend the client is not alone. Accompanied by a troupe there is greater strength, less fear that one can be hurt by the unknown barrister.

Shaking his head, turning down an offer of Starbuck's Vienna Blend, unaccompanied but obviously stressed, "here's the deal," my new client began, getting right down to business, "I've got until the 14th [two weeks from this moment] to get this done."

"What done?" I asked. He hadn't said.

"I was married for 21 years," he began. "On *my* anniversary," — [he didn't say *our*] — my wife proposed a toast." It sounded like they were celebrating with Champagne, *the* drink with which to acknowledge a happy occasion. "'Enjoy the 21st,' she announced (with raised glass, I presumed) there won't be a 22nd.' A few minutes later I was handed a summons; she had filed for divorce."

"I didn't see this coming." He was visibly tearful. "It took me twelve years to get over it." The marriage had terminated two decades ago, I learned, but it still affected him. The ectomy remained a sore wound, still inflamed, an injury that he perceived as finally cured. No, he was definitely not over his great loss. He had been impervious to his first wife's true feelings, not recognizing what must have been frequent clues, but he felt deceived by her. It was an unforeseen shock. And now he is surely untrusting, wary of relationships.

"What's happened since then?" I asked.

"After awhile I began seeing someone else." I looked at him and nodded; the message was "tell me more."

"We went together for thirteen years — but we argued all the time. She wanted to be married. What am I," she kept asking, "just your whore?"

* This chapter is endnoted. The notes can be found at the end of this chapter.

That sounded like a fair question to me. I didn't respond, just nodded, an assurance that I was listening. I was. This was getting interesting. I didn't take notes. It would be too distracting. The yellow legal pad was clean. The nod meant, keep going, and he did.

To stop what he described as their "arguments," they married. He lost his first wife whom he cared for, and now he feared that he would lose this love, too, unless this step was taken.

"I wrote up an agreement," he said somewhat apologetically, "no lawyer involved." He was still probably angry with the adversary that represented his first wife, and who arranged the summons to be served on *his* anniversary. He continued, "ten thousand to her in full settlement if we divorce, or if either of us files for one within two years; fifty thousand if we last two to five [the language didn't sound too hopeful], and after five, then whatever I have to give her." He didn't speculate on what that might be, but I sensed that he felt that he could be reamed.

Now it was clear — the 14th was the five-year anniversary. To stop what may be a greater loss than fifty thousand, he had to file for divorce by that date. He told me that his net worth was three million, that he makes thirteen per cent on his investments — one hundred seventy-five to two hundred thousand dollars in income a year — marital property in Colorado. The real estate market is high in El Paso County, lots of appreciation has accrued on his pre-marital assets — so a chunk — a big chunk could be ordered transferred to his wife if he dilly dallied — didn't file for marriage termination.

"Three million," I said — "if not your wife, who's to get it?"

"My kids and grandkids," he replied, "two kids, six grandkids, but there'll be seven by next month. Sue is eight months pregnant." Sue is apparently one of his children. He talked as though I was intimately familiar, or should be, with his family members.

"She (his wife, not yet given a name in our conversations) has three children. There'll never be grandchildren," he went on, referring to his wife's family. I didn't ask why, but assumed that it was probably because of their age. I was mildly curious but it wasn't important.

"Have you and your wife talked about what she expects from your wealth?"

"She wants her kids included. She has nothing. It'll all have to come from me. She'd like them to get a share of my estate along with my kids, and at least twelve percent."

"Well, that's clear enough. Okay, what do you want me to do?"

"Write up my will. When I die she gets thirty per cent of the income [from my total estate]. When she dies her kids divide twelve percent of what's left and my kids and grandkids get the rest." It sounded like he had in mind one big trust. Seventy percent of the income, while his wife was alive I guessed was to go to his kids. At his wife's death, 88 percent of the trust value was to go to his family and 12 percent to hers. Twelve percent times three million, that's $360,000.00, about $120,000.00 per child, I thought,

$60,000.00 each after apportioning estate taxes.

"Who pays the taxes?" I asked, but he didn't know.

"Well, we can't do it that way," I said. "You've described a QTIP[1] trust for your wife, and you've got some generation-skipping tax issues that have to be considered because you're including grandchildren as beneficiaries in your will, and your wife is lawfully entitled to half of what you have (if you've been married to each other ten years or more) if she elects to take it after you die regardless of what your will (or trust) says unless she waives this by agreement.

That, of course, is a mouthful and I didn't expect him to understand — but I was running late and he needed to know that the legal instrument that he required wasn't to be found in any nearby form book — nor as simple as his handwritten pre-marital promises had been — written by him, no doubt, on the back of an envelope or similar scratch.

"What can I do?" He almost pleaded.

"What's more important to you? Your wife or your pile of stuff?" I deliberately insulted his treasures. He needed to see them as less important than what they otherwise were to him. Time for Ozymandias.[2]

"What's your wife's name," I finally asked.

"Ellen," he replied.

It's time to consider people — to realize that property comes second — relationships first. He hadn't learned that lesson earlier and his "it's my property because I earned it," attitude cost him marriage-one — and was about to be repeated.

"Tell me about Ellen."

And so he did. A school chum, someone he had cared for when he was a high school senior, not his sweetheart, but she could have been. After his divorce, he looked her up again and the relationship was renewed.

Resentful that he didn't marry her and tiring of waiting for a commitment she had finally resorted to an ultimatum — "fish or cut bait, Jack." And so he did, four years and three hundred and fifty-one days earlier, married her, but untrusting, not until the contract was fashioned, the one with the due date included, fourteen days from now — D-Day for him. Once that passes with no divorce pleading filed, his stuff is vulnerable. In divorce or death, he might have to share it.

"Can I see her picture?" I asked. I could. Out came the wallet — a recent photo — a 69-year old beauty. She looked kind.

"This is who we're talking about? She's stunning." Pretty hair, attractively dressed. She'd prepared for this portrait. And he cared for her, told her and me that he loved her. This photo showed us both what was at stake — what he was putting on the table to lose — high stakes — a relationship at risk and it's his hand to wager. The moment for bluffing has passed. He held the cards. He could fold or play. The pot was Ellen.

The focus shifted. The appointments have backed up, but this was surgery. It wasn't about a will or trust, or a new agreement or filing or not filing for a second failed marriage. It hadn't failed. It was about the life of a 70-year old soul whose joy in life might end with a second marriage failure, doomed thereafter to an unaccompanied end—life, with solace only from grown-up children and their kids, who surely cared for him and who may or may not covet his wealth; he didn't say. It didn't matter.

#

Three million wasn't at stake anyway, only twelve per cent of that — a comparative pittance, tax deducted from it or not, a sum that he could earn before Ellen would plant the seventy-first candle on his cake.

He didn't have to make major changes in his life — tormenting changes that would cost him Ellen. She didn't seem greedy. Her request was modest, one she, in fact, should not have even been forced to state. "Treat me as a respected human being," was her first request of him. "...make me feel wanted, needed, a real part of you and you of me, evidenced by our marriage, a commitment, a recognition of our togetherness. And now, recognize me as partner. I recognize your long, hard struggle to gain wealth — much of which came before we met again and married. You've earned esteem, but honor my request, too, for dignity, to be able to see that my children — yours too in spirit — you love them, and they you — get something from *us*. I need your assurance that they will have something that I made possible — their inheritance from you, but because of me. See my need. Do this for me. Were our lives different, I would do this for you."

And I believe she would. I imagined the picture speaking. Compassion showed in her soft and pretty face. I could hear her longing eloquence to her frightened and untrusting husband as both he and I looked at her picture — a gift from her to him — one he could carry with him in its cellophane protector, in his wallet — to look at when she was not near — assurance to him that his life now included her love — and this, too, made him strong, contributed a joy that he would not otherwise have.

I gave it my all — playing her role — forcing him with her picture to see her present with us — a part of him he cannot ignore, the source of much of his vitality, committed to him, but not wholly his.

He left, still discouraged,[3] still untrusting, uncomfortable gifting outside of blood, setting himself up to play Scrooge McDuck, sitting in isolation on his basement safe filled with hoarded gold. He was about to lose a coveted relationship, someone he loved, a mate that cared for him, and her family whom he enjoyed.

He probably won't return. I was hard on him, played adversary, took his wife's side, refused to confirm that his lack of generosity was reasonable or even defendable — because it wasn't. The lesson that he had learned in life didn't call for sharing his endowment — not even with one he seemed to love, but who was still an outsider, one who had her own penniless brood that he was disinclined to aid.

"Sorry, I'm late," was certainly metaphoric. At 70 it may be too late for him to change. Values that enable sharing for most of us are learned much earlier. The undoubted compassion shared by his two wives was lost on him. He didn't copy, didn't understand, couldn't relate — all business he, and all business successes singularly his, with no time to contemplate Ozymandius. . .

"I met a traveler from an antique land
Who said: Two vast and trunkless legs of stone
Stand in the desert . . . Near them, on the sand,
Half sunk, a shattered visage lies, whose frown,
And Wrinkled lip, and sneer of cold command,
Tell that its sculptor well those passions read
Which yet survive, stamped on these lifeless things,
The hand that mocked them, and the heart that fed:
And on the pedestal these words appear:
'My name is Ozymandias, king of kings:
Look on my works, ye Mighty, and despair!'
Nothing beside remains. Round the decay
Of that colossal wreck, boundless and bare
The lone and level sands stretch far away."[4]

ENDNOTES TO ELLEN

1. Q.T.I.P.: Qualified Terminable Interest Property [Trust], a trust that defers estate taxes until the death of the surviving spouse-trust beneficiary.
2. Percy Bysshe Shelly (1792-1822), *The College Omnibus 7th*, 1951, Harcourt, Brace and Company, p. 1073.
3. "Why [am] I not of the same mind when I was a boy that I am now? . . . [W]hy do not the ruddy checks of my youth return to help me now?" Horace, Od., iv. 10, 7, Quintus Horatius Flaccus, 65-8 B.C.E., Roman lyric poet and satirist. Cited in Michel de Montaigne, "Of Repentance," *Selected Essays*, Dover Pub., N.Y., p. 65, 68.
4. *Supra*, n.2.

Postscript

Qualities of human lives are not overlooked by lawyers who come to the aid of clients whose longevity brings them to an end-life, life's last segment, a time when repair is no longer possible, when the body energy for cell replacement declines and finally ceases.

Cookies ... and *Alice* ... and *Mikki* ... are stories about people experiencing their decline, considering last acts that precede death. At this moment, Alice questioned whether or not her gifts provided for in her will to itinerant preachers who entertained her for much of her life were appropriate.

The hero and heroine in *Cookies* were certain about their choices. Mikki's friends needed reassurance that their design for themselves would not injure their children whom they still perceived as needful.

All were persons of value, nearing or in their end-life, remaining purposeful in their final schemes for the transfer of their wealth.

Ellen described a different quality, an emotional difficulty affecting personal happiness. Ellen's husband suffered with an inability to overcome a misperceived duty to provide exclusively for issue and little or nothing for a second spouse whom he cared for but continued to see as an interloper, an intruder in his life, one he loved but one who could also prevent his satisfying a perceived greater obligation, leaving his wealth to his seed and its progeny.

PART TEN

*Physiologia**

"'The trains are running late — do something!' When [his companion] replied that she didn't [see any trains] he [reacted] in anger, 'What's the matter with your eyes[;] can't you see?' and pointed down at his untied shoe laces. Suddenly, she understood. 'He just wanted me to tie his laces, but he expressed it in this [malapropos] way. He knew what he wanted to say, but he couldn't get the right words [out], and didn't even realize it.'"[1]

An inquiry into the nature of things, *physiologia*, in the Greek, confronts our scientists in their study of Alzheimer's Disease. The Greeks would describe their efforts as pathophysiological, the inquiry into the causes of suffering and disease, in the case of Alzheimer's, the study of a degrading sickness.

As elder law attorneys, we confront the current lack of success of the scientific effort, as we grieve with our demented[2] clients and their family members over the insidious, relentless and progressive life of the illness that ultimately kills our clients, and which will surely greet some of us as well.

Pathophysiological inquiry has determined that the disease is accompanied by the loss of vast numbers of cortical cells associated with memory, learning, and judgement, and by a decrease of acetylcholine, a chemical compound that transmits impulses from the brain's nerve fibers.[3] "[C]onvolutions of the brain are atrophied, separated from one another, shallowed or flattened, compressed and small, especially in the frontal region. It is not uncommon, that one or two convolutions of the convexity of the brain are depressed, and almost destroyed, and the empty space filled with serum."[4]

But the physiologia has remained unsuccessful. With Alzheimer's it has described the failing organ, but notwithstanding this awareness, no cure has been forthcoming.

* This chapter is endnoted. The notes can be found at the end of this chapter.

And now, nearing two centuries from Philippe Pinel's[5] description of this modern-day démence, "[w]e know not a whit more about what might cure it than we do about what might cause it."[6]

There are currently four million citizens in this country, and 17 to 20 million world-wide, who are affected by Alzheimer's.[7] Dementia of the Alzheimer's type, its official medical description, accounts for an estimated 50 to 60 per cent of all dementing illnesses suffered by our elder clients.[8] With the exploding elder population, estimated at 76 million Americans over age 65 years by the year 2040, without a pathophysiological success, our health care stress, deemed critical now, will certainly be exacerbated.[9]

And what are we to do? What are the appropriate roles of law and elder law advocates in this milieu? What are rational moral expectations for our clients and for ourselves with regard to publicly supported biomedical research? What objectives are reasonable for government funding aimed at prolonging death and reducing lethal disease, including Alzheimer's, for suffering older Americans — what Daniel Callahan[10] refers to as "rescue medicine,"[11] particularly in light of forecasts suggesting that illnesses present in the last stage of elders' lives "...will continue to resist treatment and defy cure?"[12]

Barbara Logue[13] suggests that medical priority be given to medical applications that benefit biographical life rather than life's biological component; and this means that, in her opinion, where there can be "...no meaningful return to the human community,"[14] financial resources should not be wastefully used even though such a choice will be death-hastening for some. Logue holds that values that affirm expenditures resulting in the prolonging of biological life alone are not preferable to death.[15]

Dramatic gains in longevity witnessed in this country in this century may continue into the next.[16] The predicted increased use of the over-the-counter hormone Melatonin, for example, may assure this.[17] If the gains in average life expectancy continue, there could be 138 million Americans older than 65 by the year 2040, "...and as many as 78 million people older than 85 [years] by 2080, 26 times more than there [were in 1993]."[18] But while science and health consciousness are increasing the longevity of our citizenry, they are not curing elders of their acute or chronic diseases. For this reason, the fear that some social scientists have is that longer lives will equate to even more sicker lives. Dr. Richard Sprott of the National Institute on Aging, quoted by Melinda Beck in a *Newsweek* special report, for example, says, "If we are able to produce 150-year-old people, but they spend 40 years in [nursing homes] we [will] have created a disaster."[19]

Notwithstanding Sprott's ominous prophecy, we must not abandon our support of biomedical research aimed at the cause and cure of Alzheimer's as well as other lethal elder diseases.[20] Such research is not only rescue medicine — available to help only those who now experience the trauma of their death-causing illnesses, extending biological life, but collaterally, this research aims at prevention as well, and Callahan, in his "Our Fear of Dying" essay[21] wrongfully calls for rationing.[22] Such a word — rationing — might be worsened by definition to mean irresponsibly terminating. He writes, " ... American hospitals and nursing homes might consider framing and putting in their lobbies the American philosopher George Santayana's reflections on death: 'The end of an evening party is to go to bed; but its use is to gather congenial people together, that they may pass the time pleasantly. An invitation to the dance is not ironical because the dance cannot last forever.'"[23]

Compare this sardonic conclusion with the more sensitive humanity of Sherwin B. Nuland, M.D., as he addresses the loss of those we love by causes of death that confuse us and those who are in death's throes, struggling with the task of dying. In *How We Die*, he writes: "There are no consolations in the diagnosis of Alzheimer's Disease. The anguish may be mitigated by good nursing care, support groups, and the closeness of friends and family, but in the end, it will be necessary for patients and loved ones together to walk through that very tortuous valley of the shadow, in the course of which everything changes forever. There is no dignity in this kind of death. [It is not gentle.] It is an arbitrary act of nature and an affront to the humanity of its victims. If there is wisdom to be found [in the suffering that this enfeebling disease causes], it [is] in the knowledge that human beings are capable of [a quality] of love and loyalty that transcends not only [this] physical debasement but [also] the spiritual weariness of the years of sorrow [for the elders and their families that accompanies life's final chapter for those who suffer and ultimately die from this dreadful and dehumanizing disease]."[24] The inquiry must continue. The cause and cure must be found.

ENDNOTES

1. Sherwin B. Nuland, *How We Die*, "Reflections on Life's Final Chapter," (Vintage, N.Y., 1995), C. 5, "Alzheimer's Disease," pp. 89, 100.
2. Philippe Pinel, a Paris physician, gave the name démence, dementia in English, to the disease that causes incoherence of mental faculties. He wrote in *Traité médico-philosophique sur l'aliénation mentale*, (1801), a description that we know now as Alzheimer's: "Rapid succession or uninterrupted alternation of isolated ideas, and evanescent and unconnected emotions [unconnected either to each other or to external real events]. Continually repeated acts of extravagance: complete forgetfulness of every previous state: diminished sensibility to external impressions: abolition of the faculty of judgement: perpetual activity." Id., p. 108.
3. *Id.*, p. 91.
4. *Id.*, p. 110. Quoting Jean Etienne Dominique Esquirol, *Des Maladies mentales*, (1838).
5. *Supra* n.2.
6. Nuland, *supra*, n.1. This may be somewhat of an exaggeration. Joan Rattner Heilman, "The Good News About Alzheimers," *Parade Magazine*, (Aug. 13, 1995), p. 12, reports that "[i]t has been found . . . that some people inherit abnormal genes, predisposing them to Alzheimer's . . . ." The search is on for drugs that may " . . . stop the flawed metabolism . . . [so that the unsuspecting gene carriers will not develop Alzheimer's;]" Marcia Barinaga, "Missing Alzheimer's Gene Found," 269 *Science*, (Aug. 18, 1995), p. 917. *And see*, Nancy L. Mace, and Peter V. Rabins, *The 36-Hour Day*, Revised edition (Johns Hopkins Un. Press, Baltimore, 1991), C. 18, "Research in Dementia," p. 291.
7. Four million who reside in the U.S. is an estimation. Id., p. 103. There are 17 to 20 million people affected by Alzheimer's worldwide. *Science, id.*
8. Id., p. 107. Elder is defined in this context as one over age 65 years.
9. *See* Melinda Beck, "The Gray Nineties," Special Report, *Newsweek*, (October 4, 1993), p. 65. "Americans over 65 make up only about 13 percent of the nation's population today, yet they account for more than one-third of all health spending. They fill 40 percent of all hospital beds and consume twice as much prescription medication as all other age groups combined. An additional 6,000 Americans turn 65 every day. That number will double when the oldest baby boomers reach retirement age, [15] years from now. The `oldest old' — those 85 and over — account for twice as much spending as those who are merely elderly, and they are growing even faster as a percentage of the population . . . . Encouragingly, recent studies at Duke have found that the rate of disabilities grew more slowly than the elderly population grew during the 1980's — an indication . . . that medical advances and

healthier lifestyles are paying off in added years of good health. But other experts warn that some of the most crippling diseases of old age, including Alzheimer's and Parkinson's, can't be staved off by exercise or dietary changes."

10. Daniel Callahan, "Our Fear of Dying — How our Determination to Control Mortality has Distorted the Mission of Medicine," *Newsweek*, (October 4, 1993), p. 67.
11. "In other industrial countries neither a very-low-birth-weight baby nor a seriously ill elderly person is likely to be subjected to aggressive treatment. They have made judgments that in certain cases the price of continued treatment is simply too burdensome to the patient and society. It is not just that we believe death is one more ailment to overcome. We also seem to believe that health care should be at the top of our domestic priority list, ahead of job creation or public education. Does it make any sense that in the past 35 years or so, we have spent more than twice as much on health care as we have on education?" Id., p. 67.
12. Barbara J. Logue, *Last Rights — Death Control and the Elderly in America*, (Macmillan, N.Y., 1993), p. 290, citing James F. Fries and Lawrence M. Crapo, *Vitality and Aging: Implications of the Rectangular Curve*, (W. H. Freeman, San Francisco, 1981), p. 93.
13. *Id.*, p. 292.
14. *Id.*
15. *Id.*, p. 293. Logue refers to this as "gentle death."
16. *Supra*, n.9, p. 65
17. Geoffrey Cowley, "Melatonin," *Newsweek*, (August 7, 1995), p. 46. "It's the hot . . . hormone [which] could reset the body's aging clock, turning back the ravages of time."
18. *Supra*, n.9, p. 65.
19. *Id.*
20. Funding for research and age—related illnesses throughout the National Institute of Health is only about, "700 million [dollars] this year. That is less than three-tenths of one percent of the 340 billion [dollars] spent on caring for older Americans." Id., p. 66.
21. *Supra*, n.10, p. 67.
22. *See* Chapter 13, "Disposable Humanity."
23. *Supra*, n.10, p. 67.
24. *Supra*, n.1., p. 117.

*"An Agony that Will Never Heal"**

"I don't break for lawyers." This pithy aphorism was printed in large letters on the bumper of an old, smashed up car parked in front of me. Its driver was impatient. We were both waiting for the red light that controlled our lane to change, allowing us to move on. Viewing the car's decrepit body and listening to its driver's incessant revving of its engine, I suspected that he didn't break for anybody.

During this long wait, I imagined that the driver's dislike of lawyers was occasioned by having, in his mind, been creamed by one. He was probably divorced, I assumed, and his long-suffering wife must have received a fair share of the booty; she wasn't deserving, in his opinion, and he's still mad. Revving the engine no doubt helps.

There's not much to do while we're alone, waiting out a long red one, except to let our minds and memories entertain us. And that's what I was doing — entertaining myself until the amber and green appeared.

Our minds give our lives cohesion, our memories and our awareness of ourselves in our experiences. Memories are our personal encyclopedias. As we age, they are the growing foundations for our present experiences. Memory gives us continuity as we lope through our personal histories.

This is what is taken from the Alzheimer's victim. This fundament of individual lives is something that medicine and physicians, families and lawyers cannot retrieve for them. There is no remedy when the cortex of a once firm and agile brain becomes like an irrelevant computer, not yet discarded, but no longer working its imperial magic.

Lawyers are sometimes consulted when a family member's grief over the loss of a once strong family patrician overwhelms them. They know that there is no help beyond what the physician has sympathetically told them, and beyond what they've read, but they need to be heard, to grieve out loud, and to tell someone whom they view as caring what has happened in their lives, a part, now, of their memories, and indelibly so. And, we listen to their agony which will never fully heal.

"He sees things that are not there, stands by the window and looks out. He paces. He thinks that there are people in our home, strangers, and they've stolen his razors.

"He believes that sometimes these strangers sleep in our bed, and so he sleeps on the couch, and I sleep by him on the floor.

"He left the house at 2:00 a.m. the other night, said he was 'going home.' I followed him and asked if he would postpone this trip until morning, but he wouldn't wait. I

* This phrase is from Oliver Sacks, M.D., *The Man Who Mistook His Wife for a Hat*, chapt. 2, "The Lost Mariner," pp. 23, 42, describing Korsakou's Syndrome, "... a profound and permanent ... devastation of memory ...."

hurried back inside and called 911. Two police came and rescued him.

"This came on suddenly after his driver's license wasn't renewed, and just after my mastectomy. These two events hit him hard and he's never recovered.

"Some days he knows me; some days he doesn't. I have him in a home now, twelve patients are there, $1,600 a month. The R.N. isn't always around and then he doesn't get his meds. I stayed until 8:00 last night. He's to have his medicine at 6:00. He never got it. The R.N. never came."

She paused and looked away, picturing in her mind, I supposed, her fallen hero. "He shuffles now. I don't know what to do."

It was a long monologue; my distressed client was unloading — and I listened. And that's all each of us could do. She could talk, expose her awful grief; her lawyer could listen, absorbing part of her pain. The abyss in which the Alzheimer patient lives is shared by those who love him (or her). For one of them, time has terminated,[1] memory is erased; for the other, grief, sometimes insufferable, dominates her waking and sleeping moments. Both await the "final amnesia ... 'the one that can erase an entire life.'"[2] For this once close and loving couple, it is "an agony that will never heal."

ENDNOTES

1. Oliver Sacks, (referred to at the foot of the first page of this story), footnote, p. 31, quoting the prolific author, Studs Terkel, in a conversation with the author. "I never met anyone for whom time [has] terminated," Terkel said. If he wishes to suffer this experience, a third stage Alzheimer's victim, one found in any nearby nursing home who accepts dementia patients, can accommodate him. It will measurably affect him and, consciously or not, influence his writing as well.
2. *Id.*, p. 33, quoting Luis Bañuel's recently translated memoirs.

Postscript

Perhaps its inception begins in our sixties when we can't instantly recall the name of a friend. The name eventually is retrieved and perhaps only a few seconds may have passed, but our body's computer is slow in processing it, slower than the quick recall inherent in our past, and we are aware of this reality.

We are less embarrassed about the momentary memory failure in whatever context it occurs than what we fear is the introduction of Alzheimers — phase one — into our lives. We joke about it, but we are aware that our personal computer isn't working with its historic efficiency, and if there has been Alzheimers in the family, we wonder if we are experiencing the work product of a gene — one of four now believed to participate in familial Alzheimers, the dreaded dementia. This concern exacerbates the problem; the anxiety makes more difficult timely summoning of the misplaced name.

Lawyers who work with elders listen to the moaning of family members who make appointments to get their ancestor's affairs in order while the aged one is still sufficiently competent to execute documents necessary for others to act as their agents when (not if) the disease impairs their loved one's ability to make and communicate responsible decisions for themselves.

It may not be Alzheimers, but that's what the family calls it. A dementing disease is destroying the strong family leader by whatever name.

The lawyer is not the first professional seen by the family. The doctor is first, or perhaps, in deeply religious families, the pastor. By the time the family's legal counselor is seen, there is little question that dementia, in some form, by whatever name it ultimately will be called, has forever changed the once strong noble's character.

At this juncture in an elder's life, powers of attorney (durable agencies) are, more frequently than not, no longer options. The elder's capacity is too diminished. Guardians of the person and conservators, protectors of the elder's wealth, appointed by the court, must now be turned to as aides, fiduciaries of last resort. Family denial lasted too long, and less intrusive authority in the form of trusts or agencies requiring the ill one's signature for approval are no longer possible.

"Physiologia" expresses the problem, "An Agony That Will Never Heal," the consequence.

PART ELEVEN

"I Think That's Why I'm Not Dead Yet"

"You know, I'm 85?"
This was the greeting from Myvestra
as I walked into my client's home.
It was summer and the front door
was left open for me.

"Yes, I know that," I responded to this odd opening line. "And I'm still bossy. I don't know why. I just order everyone around."

Momentarily contemplative, Myvestra loudly inhaled through her oxygen lifeline. It was affixed to a cannister 30 feet or so away, established as a not-too-be-moved fixture located at the mid-point in her home's long hallway. The heavy tank had compressed the carpeting beneath it into an indented, permanent circle.

"I think that's why I'm not dead yet," she reasoned after this loud, long gasp enriched her blood. "The Lord must not need another officer." — or even a three-striper I silently thought.

In earlier days Myvestra would have leaned back and laughed, "at my funny," as she would say, imagining herself as an officer, but she's hunched over now, dependent upon a walker and her still strong upper arms to move about. Leaning in any direction even when sitting is out of the question. She'll lose her balance and fall, and she knows that, so she limited herself to a wry smile and eyed my face for a reaction.

Upon entering her home, I had followed Myvestra's "snake," the long oxygen tubing affixed to the life supporting cannister in the hallway into her back bedroom. She was sitting in a chair by a window facing southwest. It overlooked Fareway Eight on the neighboring golf course, one whose rough abutted her lot line. Shooting east from the tee, a golfer would need to be burdened with a horrible hook to result in the dimpled whim-wham ending up in her yard, and an even worse hook for a Titilest missile to tap her window. "It's never happened," she said, "no ball buzzing in my yard." She even knew the caddies' lingo.

The back bedroom, the one used by Myvestra's occasional house guests, but mostly by Myvestra herself, as her sitting room, even in her younger days, was where I invariably found her. She spent her days beside the room's large pane, her personal telescope, which made the life passing by each day in search for the green ending Fareway Eight, seem nearer and larger than it really is. She enjoyed the happiness she witnessed in the golfers walking by. Their bright colored clothes amused her, and in the summer months when her window was opened, she'd hear words she hadn't heard since the previous summer. "Holy Damn," she said, "What does that mean?" I shrugged my shoulders.

Myvestra had, until recently, been imprisoned in one of our city's nursing homes — unable to leave without her doctor's orders and the physician was hesitant to risk his patient's return to her home. On life-sustaining oxygen full time, he wanted to know whether her kitchen stove was gas fueled, whether she had a fireplace that might, if used, ignite the life-saving oxygen, the O_2 on which Myvestra relied, the combustible that flowed through the long plastic tubing which trailed every step my client took. It was her permanent leash, tethering her to a tall cylindrical pole from which life-giving vapors flowed. But with it she could move about and her physician was cautious, aware of the volatile mix of oxygen and fire which she might encounter.

So Myvestra engaged a local life care agency, arranged to replace her gas powered range with a table-top micro-wave, one she could safely operate. It was placed by her refrigerator, a unit she called her "ice box," a holdover from her child-life memories when huge cubes of ice would be delivered to her parents' home each day, the fuel which kept "the cold things cold," and which necessitated emptying the drip catcher several times a day, as the large cube warmed and slowly released its fluid into a pan on the floor hidden beneath the unit. On days when the emptying duty was forgotten, "the floor got washed," she said.

#

"Twenty-four hour care." This was her doctor's requirement if Myvestra was to leave the nursing home, something that the life care agency also provided. At $12.50 an hour, this cost is $300.00 a day, and in a 30-day month, that's $9,000.00. Her release from the nursing home didn't come cheap.

As Myvestra improved and could ambulate within her home's confines, however, lesser care was needed, and after three months and the payment of $27,000.00 in 24-hour care costs, she now managed her life with four hours a day in-home care, two hours in the morning when her breakfast and lunch are prepared, and her home tidied, and two more hours, 4:00 to 6:00 in the evening when she is helped to bathe, and her dinner is made. The cost at $12.50 an hour is $50.00 a day, $1,500.00 a month, an expense that her budget can tolerate. And she has a life line, worn as a necklace, "my pearls," is her description of the device, handy to use if she does fall and become in need of emergency aid. "I'll never use it," she defiantly asserts whenever the benefit the life line provides is mentioned. "It's a waste," she mutters — but she doesn't take it off, she just wants all who will listen to understand that she's in charge, still an officer and in command of her own life.

She remains independent, and adamantly ignores the limitations which her failing health have introduced. Strapped to a cannister, held up by a walker, equipped with a life line, she's still alive, alert, lively, in touch with her environs, defiantly in control of her destiny. With worn out lungs she knows that death is near, that her officer skills will be needed by the "Great One," some day, probably soon. And she's ready, but in the meantime, she'll be listened to; her instructions will be followed and her self-esteem will continue receiving the regular nourishment it needs.

"That's why I'm not dead yet." Insightful and accurate, Myvestra won't give in. Without bitterness she tolerates what's required of her to survive, but she won't recline any time the sun is up, and she won't watch "the soaps." No stasis for her. She'll continue to absorb the stimulation she encounters in her small universe, and joyfully receive the salutes of others, those who do her bidding. She knows why she's bossy — because it works — and it works because those she orders around respond to her spiritedness and are refreshed by her love of life. She still feels needed here. She hasn't given up.... That's why she's not dead yet.

"I've Got My Money's Worth"

Whatever else may be discussed with elderly clients, one topic is never avoided. Our clients may not go into detail, but give them an opening — "how's your health?" for example, and they will tell us, most often more than we want to know.

The long list of health deficiencies of our older clients is sometimes frightening, and as some walk through our office front door, we wonder how they made it from the parking garage to the elevator, ten floors up to the law office suite. "We make home visits," they're told, but pride for many is as important, or more so, than comfort. Unless they are bedridden, or legitimately homebound, many look forward to the outing and they want to see their lawyer's office and place faces with names, in particular the appointment secretary who schedules their visits.

Bernard was such a client. In his early 70's, he was a bit shaky and used an attractive, slender, highly polished walking stick for support. He was well-groomed, wore a starched shirt and a freshly pressed suit. A square of silk peeked out from his breast pocket, perfectly folded, in a shade that presented a pleasant contrast to his demure tie. "Spiffy," I'd call his dress, rakish; I told him so.

My client, however, was ill, "terminally so" were his words, and our meeting was scheduled to wrap up his affairs, get his papers in order and plan for a distribution of his worldly goods.

In large letters, *Pre-Mortem Planning* appears on the spine of the text we look to in preparation for these meetings. None of the books ready us, however, for the tension indigenous to such a conference. The undercurrent of grief felt by family members who are bravely enduring the hopeless wait — the fateful, tragic end of life of one among them, one loved and cherished, testaceous as they appear, is deadly. And these family onlookers are often unable to maintain their starchy demeanor.

My client looked so healthy, it was difficult to conceive that his life was nearly over. There is a tendency, of course, to deny hopeless realities, to buoy the feeling of those facing their own ill health and probable soon-to-come death. We need to be careful not to promise them that they're going to get better.

"I'm not used to getting ready to die every day," my client spoke quietly, looking, while he spoke, directly at me. I blinked.

"You've got a lot of life to live yet!" I quickly reacted, and the message sounded to me to be too close to "you're going to get better." This isn't true. We both knew it, and Bernard didn't need to hear any more euphuisms. There was silence. I didn't know what to say, but my understanding client rescued me. It was my turn to be buoyed. "I've got my money's worth," he said, and his eyes twinkled. I'm okay was his meaning. I've accepted this reality. I've had a good life. I'm preparing for the event. Certainly Bernard has responded similarly to others who attempted to rescue his feelings and bolster his remaining hope. "I've got my money's worth." Perfect! It diffused the tension and now we could move on to the mundane — reviewing the Will, the title to assets, the advance directives, the financial agencies, the possibility of estate reduction by gifting, the funeral arrangements and the data needed for the death certificate — the pre-mortem checklist routine.

"Pets?" I asked.

"My piebald cat," he answered.

"Piebald?" I repeated.

He eyed my 1,765 page *Oxford Encyclopedic Dictionary* on its stand covering a large section of the space on the left side of my desk behind us. We sat at a round table to the left of my work space.

"Look it up," he suggested. He was having fun with me. The banter helped.

We took care of "Piebald." I never did get the feline's actual name — perhaps "Piebald" is it. On the tangible property memorandum, identifying specific gifts that were to be made following his death, he wrote, "my piebald cat" in lower case letters followed by the donee's name — the one who would feed, house and enjoy this special member of Bernard's family. He was still teasing. The twinkle remained in his eyes.

What a grand man. Near death, he dressed for what we both expected would be the final meeting with his lawyer — an important outing for him, one worth the fuss. He took care of everything, signed the new documents we prepared while he waited, reflecting his current values, persons he wanted to benefit; we changed a few names here and there, put the new documents in a handy folder for him and closed it. The work's done. It's time for the client to leave. It had been a long afternoon; time now to return home to rest — to give Piebald a treat — snoozing with his master on top of the bed until dinnertime.

"You've got a lot of life to live left" turned out not to be a harmful remark. He was full of life — not many days to enjoy it — but in those days left, he intended to continue the joy he obviously gets from living. His pride in self, inspiring him to dress rakishly when he leaves his home, his teasing banter, his foresightful preparations to ease his family's transition to life without him, without remorse, without blame, without requesting pity — all evidence of an exceptional member of the human community whom I was privileged to know.

He loved his life; it has been relatively long. Death now or later, he got his money's worth.

Postscript

Unless we are in great and constant pain, most of us don't give up our interest in life. We accommodate to our restrictions. Healthy, in our earlier years, we find it difficult to imagine living in a significantly restricted environment, such as being confined to bed, or attached to an oxygen canister. We bravely spurt to anyone who is listening that in such condition, we would not want our lives continued. "Pull the Plug" is the aphorism we voice. And, we are no doubt serious when we speak in this manner. (*See* Chapter 15, "Because I Like It Here.") "I've Got My Money's Worth" is somewhat of an aberration. Near death, Bernard had accepted this reality, and Myvestra found life attached to an oxygen canister not as oppressive as she, no doubt, at an earlier time imagined it would be.

Life's not over even when the diagnosis is terminal. We still cope, still hope, accommodating ourselves to this new adventure, joyless as it may be.

PART TWELVE

Living Art

A small adobe home, dirty white with blue accents surrounding two small windows, old and enduring stood picturesque at the top of a steep incline, 100 yards north of the one-lane dirt road where I'd parked my car. It was precisely 3:00 o'clock and my client, a tiny 92-year-old widow, was standing in its doorway, leaning on a walker, the kind that has wheels on its front pedestals. A cell phone was laying in a basket-carrier strapped onto the front brace. She was waiting for me, and had her phone with her in the event I called to cancel.

"You could have driven up," she said as I approached, but that was not the instruction she had given to me by phone earlier that day. "Park on the dirt road," she'd said, "and walk up the hill to the adobe. Don't go to the big house to the west," she'd instructed. The great house was used only for storage these days. It held her large art collection — one numerous charities in the city knew about and coveted.

Her two homes were hidden on 37 acres of hilly, rocky soil north of the state university, a homestead she'd purchased after leaving Indiana soon after her graduation from college there. She'd built the adobe in which she now lived. But that was long ago, near three quarters of a century, and now the tiny hovel, suffering from both age and inattention looked humble, and appeared unsafe.

"Take the interstate until you reach High Bluffs Parkway, turn right, east, until you see Vulture Haven Road; it's gravel. Go three-quarters of a mile north until you come to the three branches in the road. Take the left branch. It's a dirt road; go a few hundred yards until you see my place." At that point she'd told me to park on the single lane in front of her home — the adobe — and walk up the hill. I obeyed. She'd given clear instructions confidently, and had obviously described this same route to others. She has it down pat. The "branches" she described, however, were not like a three-hole candelabra. The first branch, wandering northward was a full block from the second, a roadway to the right which headed back in the direction of the city. I didn't continue forward to find the third, but rather headed back to the first turn, branch one, I assumed. Why hadn't she said, "Take the first left?" It had been more than awhile since she'd been on the road, I imagined, and she'd compressed the distance among these options in her memory. It's time again for her to revisit the long dirt road entrance to her home and recompose the instructions. But I'd left the office early knowing of my own navigational deficiencies, so I wasn't late.

Inside the adobe was one large room. It held a stained hardwood table, her desk, where she read and took her meals. Condiments and a rather new deck of playing cards and piles of mail, her filing arrangement for letters she couldn't discard, took up most of the table's surface, but she'd cleared a space for me, room enough for my yellow legal pad.

My client's bed was three feet to the right of the table-desk and was being used today, at least, as an extension of the hardwood. Small piles of papers that I might ask to see were laid neatly on the blanket that served also as the spread.

The home's single room contained a small refrigerator and an apartment-size stove. Two baskets of canned goods were on the floor; stove, refrigerator and the larder were all in a windowless nook that jutted out from what was otherwise a small, rectangular house, behind and to the right of the desk, her kitchen space. A closed door near the bed I surmised was the home's bath. An overstuffed chair was to the right of the door. But that's all there was. From where I was seated I could see everything in the home, and it looked to me like a perfect playhouse for a child. There were a few pictures nailed onto the walls, but nothing I would call art, and certainly nothing that mirrored the photographs of the art collection that decorated the main house. The photos had been recently taken by the appraiser. His report, a thick volume, perhaps two inches in an 8_ x 11 notebook, was on the bed. We looked at the photographs and I enjoyed her collection vicariously, as did she. It is now impossible for her to make her way down the hill to the dirt drive, and up another stony grade to the home where she and her husband had lived — the hideaway for her precious collection. The photographs and her memories were enough now. I saved for another visit the story she must have about the art. She made no offer to discuss it. Her existing will provided for its next home — a provision that was to be reaffirmed in the draft of what may, in truth, really be her Last Will, the one I am now to create. Lifetime gifts of the paintings to her charities which would result in income tax benefits to her now were not broached; her paintings, hoarded in the big house were her still—infant children. For undiscussed and not disclosed reasons it was obvious to me that her great prizes, notwithstanding their vulnerability to loss if kept in the now abandoned two-story — were not to be disturbed. "Insured?" I asked. But she didn't answer, and changed the subject; I resolved to put this in a letter to her, perhaps the one that will accompany the will draft. I suspect that it's the expense; she knows the cost of insuring valuable art, but the option to gift the paintings now is unpalatable, forcing as it would, a recognition of her own mortality because the art is not to be disturbed before she dies, and the discomfort that follows one's own children leaving home that she would experience. Her brood is not yet mature — not ready to be separated from her. Given now, their susurration would be gone and her life would be different. In her simple little hovel-house the knowledge that her art is nearby, not gone, still needing her protection, is comforting, and gives her life purpose.

Her *children* require her vicarious attention, her patronage, the protection that she gives them in her large, private safe-box, the big house, close to her, near her watchful eye.

Her importance is identified with her possessions, her prizeful art, and childless, she sees her paintings as though they are animate, requiring her attention, valuable to her, not solely because of their intrinsic worth, but because they are hers, and as time has passed, others have become attracted to them and want them, but that moment, the time when they leave her home — is hers to control and will be measured by the date of her death.

Her *children* are like jewels in her private safe, unworn, unseen — sightlessly retained, and the knowledge that they are hers is sustaining. They belong to her alone and only she can hear their quiet whispers. Intimacy with them, touching, fondling, and caressing them is unnecessary. Possession alone, knowing they are hers is enough.

We finished viewing the art book, the photographs of her great collection of magnificent paintings. She closed the notebook's cover, in which the image of each painting was protected with clear cellophane, and she closed the cover with great pride. She is putting her children to bed — an obvious metaphor. The book had been open when I arrived.

I smiled at the tiny one. Perhaps 70 pounds, or maybe 80, my client is thin. She's wearing a clean house dress and Reeboks. Her white hair is braided into two pigtails, tied with rubber bands about an inch above the stubs. These ends are rounded like inverted Japanese fans, not straight cut, but in semi-circles, laying on each side of her neck and accenting her pretty face. "You are a picture," I said. "Living, art," she replied smiling, and she was not alone referring to herself — a bright one, she.

Walter Mitty

"I had to keep running up and down the field," the one I call the poet told me. He had done that and won the game. He was a hero, and he described his artful running over and over. The crowds were cheering and his team had won, and it was because of him that this triumph was celebrated.

The caregiver had turned on the t.v., I suspect, and the poet was forced to watch a football game, something I have never seen him do. He has always hated football — sports of all kinds, really. He was no athlete, a small man, he topped out before shrinkage began at 5'4". That he wasn't taller was a constant embarrassment to him, and he equated all sports figures as much taller and larger than he, and perhaps for this reason, he didn't care for them. Even though he could have participated in athletic activities not requiring height or bulk, he didn't. He disliked them all.

An "A" student in school notwithstanding that his father would not allow him to read or study at home — his father hated school — he managed and was perhaps stimulated by study being forbidden. He'd received straight A's in high school, except for one semester. In one class, he'd gotten an "F." It was, of course, in gym.

Now redeemed, at 93, he'd gotten the ball, the pigskin. For one afternoon, he was a great running back, one on whom his team relied, and he was back in school again, on the team, its featured runner, the class hero, the scholar athlete.

"I had to keep running up and down the field," he told me again. "They (presumably his classmates) were cheering. I had the ball and we won."

#

The poet is the great entertainer of late. With a twinkle in his eye and without concision of speech, he describes events unrelated, I believe, to his own history. His imagination is rich and allows no infelicity in expressing indulgent fantasies.

I stopped by the poet's home. It was early evening, and I'd brought freshly baked cheese bread and hot apple tortes. "He won't keep his pants on," the caregiver told me as I walked in. He was sitting in his wheelchair in the middle of the living room, center stage, "naked as a jaybird" below his waist, getting ready perhaps for a post-game shower.

"Better put your shorts on, poet. There's a lady in the house." So, after coaxing, he stood and one by one slipped his legs into his boxers and I pulled them up. He sat down again so I made no attempt to try this again with his slacks. There was no reason to double cover anyway. "Why do the shorts keep coming off?" I asked. He looked away without answering. It didn't matter or it was none of my business. "Dumb question," I surmised.

"Was the poet in the army?" the caregiver asked. "He's been telling me about his combat flights." No aide-de-camp he, a pilot, no less! This 93 year old was not in the service and certainly not a flyer. What an imagination he was demonstrating. "Tell me about your army days," I suggested, but I received no response. The woo was over. The interest in fame for the moment had passed. The poet was busily gnawing on a piece of toasted cheese bread. His whole attention was being given to that. "Like the bread?" I asked, but he didn't respond, didn't even look up. Our conversation for the moment was over. The poet was dining, enjoying the hot bread, savoring it along with the Starbucks® special blend his caregiver had just brewed.

Perhaps the heroic anecdotes will be resumed, more description of extravagant daydreams, his imagined personal triumphs related, but no more tonight. Now it's time for the post-game feast, and all of the poet's energy and interest are concentrated on this evening's special gastronomic treat.

"He's making all of these stories up," his caregiver uncritically exclaimed. And, of course, he is; but isn't perception reality? Shouldn't we encourage the self-esteem his unseen periapt makes possible? No *heroi*-comic, the poet's memory is ambitious, grand, bold. On his stage he plays singular hero, and his memory esteems him. He is a person of importance. His extravagant daydreams of his imagined triumphs makes his end life romanticized, unreal but energizing, visions which he can share with those who care for him.

#

"I had to keep running up and down the field. I had the ball, and we won, and everyone was cheering!"

Indeed we are! Keep running, poet.... Keep running.

Postscript

Observing a client in his or her own home introduces a perspective unnoticed in the sanctity of our office suites. There we can only imagine what our clients' lives are like; we're dependent upon what they tell us. There is nothing that we can observe about their habitats, their style of living, extrinsic to what they voice about themselves. In our clients' homes, we may observe matters of importance. Our clients are often more verbal on their own turf where they feel comfortable. They show their sanctum to us; they're usually proud of it. Regardless of the clients' age or incapacity, their home is frequently spotless; when they know that we're coming by, they prepare for the occasion.

This is what "Living Art" is about — a wealthy client's hovel, a home where she feels comfort surrounded by very little, with her private museum in the dwelling beside her cottage, filled with valued art for which she is docent.

A lawyer with an elder law practice, somewhat like a small town physician, those docs who in our country's early formation went where their clients could be found, bedside in their homes. Some doctors do that even today and in every state in this country, lawyers with elder law practices, similarly are standing by their clients' bedsides, addressing legal concerns, matters of importance, making their clients' end-lives less anxious, confirming that the transfers of the elders' wealth will occur as planned, and that designated agents will make helpful decisions using durable agencies (powers of attorney for financial matters and health care decision-making) which their lawyers have prepared when and if their clients' ability to be fully self-reliant has ended.

Final Surprise

"My daughter and I have had many discussions about angels being here on earth. You might be pleased to know that she is right."

This was the whole of the letter. It was signed by its author and placed in a sealed envelope and enclosed in a book, one from her personal library, one she knew her lawyer would enjoy.

This client hid her message in a text, stuffed snugly between a thin Penguin paperback's mid pages, aligned lengthwise with its spine. For this moribund writer, the brief note was the last communication to her lawyer, carefully drawn, a unique, unexpected expression of gratitude, an imaginative thank you, a delightful surprise.

#

"Do you want his books?"

The listener's father, "Papa" to his family, the "poet" to the listener, was a retired clergyman, and he had just recently died. His daughter was in charge of clearing his home of its detritus, accumulated over the poet's lifetime.

There was little to salvage. Any item of value had been gifted earlier. At 94, the poet was confined to a hospital bed in what was once his den, the room in which he wrote, where his sermons and poems were crafted; and as evidence of his fertile and imaginative mind, where, more than two decades earlier, an occasional science fiction piece was penned as well. The copyrights on the poet's imaginative works had matured and Star Trek® enthusiasts now find his dramatic visions on the Internet. They're being republished by "trekkies."

#

There weren't many books, perhaps 30; all had been well used, most of them underlined here and there, underscoring ideas he might want to refer to later. The horizontal yellow lines made by the marker were old by decades and appeared now as faded beige. Several of the volumes had covers nearly separated from their texts. The print type in most of these volumes I'd call mini-pica, requiring a magnifying lens to read. Their owner, however, was uncomplaining, and his age-wizened eyes and his magnifier made out their meaning.

A dense *Merriam-Websters*, 3350 pages, second "epochal" edition, published in 1934, its face cover and spine gone, lay atop the large box in which the books had been placed. The remaining flap on the backside of the *Websters* remained precariously attached to its flyleaf. The pages of lexicography, those on which the words are defined, seemed to be intact, but the Forward, the book's prefatory explanation of what this lexicon is about, is missing, and its last century definitions are now, for the most part, archaic. There are no modern idioms described in this text like those infecting our current speech, such as "you know," "I mean" and "basically." This glossary's best years, like its owner, had passed. Except as a reminder of our country's changing and expanding language, it didn't seem like a keeper — but, of course, the listener took it.

#

Who doesn't harbor things in books — clippings that must be saved for which one has no handy file; sometimes even money and checks are hidden within the sheathe, protected there for retrieval later — unless forgotten. Sometimes the hiding place encases a memory, a note or message saved for another day, an expression of importance, hidden, to be disclosed to the intended recipient later, a gift that, if forgotten, secured in its shelter, will be delivered, but unfortunately at a time when thanks can no longer be given to its author. Intended or not, the hidden message expresses the writer's final word.

#

The large *Websters* was held by its edges, a few sheets that once abutted the book's now missing front cover and the flyleafs that followed the alphabet's last letter. With this two—handed grip, the book's yellowed but remaining pages were shaken, and, whether planned or not, the poet's hidden verse penned on fragile scrap, now loosened from the thick text's muscular hold, fell to the floor; its tribute is tearfully read.

To my son, July 16, 1977

Someone asked him what grace a man might receive
Which would more than compensate
For the rigors and hurts and disappointments that are so
Overwhelming in this enigma of existence.

And he replied: I can answer in full truth
For I have received it
Even though I cannot show it, describe it
Nor measure, nor proclaim it
But I can tell you what it is
And if you are wholly a man
You can understand it.

The priceless gift that a man might hope to receive
Is the gift of needing to look upward
Always upward
In order to see the full stature of that other man
Who is his son.

This verse was a private surprise read quietly by a stunned son who was privileged to once again hear, from the typewritten words, the voice of his father. And in case it had not been well expressed during the poet's lifetime, it was an assurance to the younger man of the patriarch's pride in his boy, now grown, himself a father, who had reached the status of a Man in his father's eyes. Announcing this to his son nearly a quarter of a century after its writing, saved and savored for this perfect moment, was his father's final surprise.

POSTSCRIPT

School Is Out — School Is Just Beginning.

When a senior law student successfully concludes the required studies at the university, and has passed the final tests necessary for graduation, one remaining barrier separates the student from an entry-level job in the profession — the state bar exam.

It's not an easy chore to pass, and in some jurisdictions less than half of those who attempt it fail on their first try. It's a difficult multiple-subject test and follows a minimum of seven years of schooling following the haunting chorus of Lohengrin's "Pomp and Circumstance." For many, the years between this moment and the tearful parting from one's adolescent companions which follows moving the tassel from the right side to the left on the high school graduation mortarboard, is more than seven. Many law school graduates have received other degrees following college matriculation, before law school enrollment. More than a smattering of gray highlights the hairstyles of scholars with whom those in the law school class compete. Diverse experiences and academic interests bring depth to class discussions which the law students' varying backgrounds make possible.

The Kansas bar exam was a two-day affair, requiring a response to a long series of short answer questions. It essentially required the 40 or so of us who sat for this test to identify the principle issue each question assumed and to relate it, in a brief reasoned analysis, to what rule of law applied. Only one of our number, principally University of Kansas and Washburn University law graduates, failed what, at least in retrospect, seemed to be an easy exam, simplistic problem solving emphasizing rules of law. The six minutes time allowed to answer each question avoided thoughtful analysis, and the consideration of options that might apply.

The Kansas exam was held in the State Supreme Court's Great Room. Nine leather chairs behind the long bench, elevated several feet above the floor below where tables and chairs had been placed for most of the exam-takers, were quickly claimed by those of us aggressive enough to seek their comfort. The nine of us claimed them on day two of the test as well, but they were not, as harbingers, announcing an event to follow. As far as I know, none of us who sat in the highbacks, assigned to the justices of the Kansas Supreme Court have been robed, and our moment of imagined glory, feeling superior to those on the gallery floor below us, was short lived. When the two-day test was over we were out of there, and the impressive leathers were reclaimed, no doubt, by the jurists.

#

"Passed" — one word on an enveloped card given to each of us on day three or perhaps four, but a short time after the two-day test was completed. Thirty-nine of us lined up to autograph the 1963 section of the Registry of Kansas Lawyers, a book kept dutifully by the Clerk of the Kansas Supreme Court. It announced on each of its completed pages, beginning, I suspect, near the date of statehood, those entitled to practice before the courts staffed with Kansas judges. Frightened, as we penned in our names, we were presumably ready. We'd passed the test. We had the 3x5s to prove it. Thereafter, for the first few years of our practices, in front of very patient judges, and with equally patient clients beside us, as young law graduates, we learned what the practice of law meant as our post-graduate education began.

My father took my picture standing on the statehouse steps. I looked as important and responsible as I possibly could. I was 28, finally out of school — no more graduation march melodies. I was bright-eyed and bushy tailed, ready to face the world.

But the tests were not over. From the Topeka state capitol steps I left for the train yards, a daily stop for the Atchison, Topeka and Santa Fe Railroad, and headed for Denver. The tests for the Colorado state bar began the following day. I had another exam to take.

A dozen and a half rectangular tables, four feet by six, were lined up in a large room in a Colorado state office building across from the state capitol. Four students were assigned to each table and after a morning of questions about personal ethics, three solid days of complex, multiple-issue case problems were given to us to resolve, individually, written in longhand in test books provided to us. New writing books and new problems were distributed periodically throughout the 24 hours of writing. We all avoided liquids. Only one examinee could leave the room at a time, he or she escorted to and from the *toilette*.

It was a tough table, the one assigned to me. A practicing M.D., a graduate engineer, a contemplative young man appearing to be quite bright, and myself. Three of us wrote furiously. He, the contemplative one, to my right, thoughtfully considered the questions and eventually would write in his test books before the loud periodic instruction to put our pencils down was commanded, but he was surely intimidated by our ferocity. He failed. The others, the three of us, were ranked first, second, and fourth among the test takers. I was fourth, intimidated, too, perhaps by the education and achievements my highly educated colleagues seated beside me possessed. There was no discussion during the breaks. Everyone was quiet, not even much eye-contact. We were all worried that we might not pass. Friendships would be renewed and new friendships begun, but not until the exams were over.

When five o'clock came, the fourth day of the exam, school was out. Eye contact was reestablished. The group was gleeful, if only because the test was over, and now for the next four months until the test results would be announced, we would remain anxious, alarmed by the consuming fear that we did not pass.

#

Now I had a home to rent. A job was already promised in Colorado Springs, a mountain town, home of Pikes Peak and Cheyenne Mountain, the latter in the process of being hollowed out for NORAD, the North American Air Defense Command. Two small ones, age four and one about four months, were being cared for by their mother, still housed in Topeka, until I could get us a rental in what was to be our new domicile. My son Stephen, four years old, asked me to get a red house with a fireplace. Those were his parting words to me. I needed to find one fast.

I met new friends on the steps of the Colorado state office building, in Denver, all from what soon was to be my hometown, Colorado Springs, and one had a car, so we rode together south on Highway 25, headed for the Springs. It was the third try in the exam for one of our group, an anxious man, near 40, bright, but pessimistic. He was hurting. One's esteem is affected by two prior failures, and two special petitions to the state Supreme Court to allow him to try again. He was sure he had failed once more following his third effort, and he was morose as well as contemplative and rigidly still. He was no doubt going over his answers to the tough problems the exam required us to analyze and resolve. His home was the first stop. He got out. We said our goodbyes — final ones it turned out; his heart gave out. He died about two weeks later — before, of course, the list was published of those who had passed. There would have been no more petitions by him for a reprieve, no need to be tested again. He had made it. He died a lawyer, one of us.

#

"I need a rental," I announced to a Colorado Springs realtor, one my new boss, the law firm's senior partner, had sent me to. "Get in," the housing guy told me, as he opened the right front door of a '63 Buick, and I did. We headed north on Tejon, a beautiful and quiet north—south street that requires a jut around Colorado College, "CC," to the locals. It sits on a square that causes Tejon to become a dead end six blocks from downtown. So we jutted, got around the college, back on Tejon, and pulled over in front of 2011. This was to be our new home — one my wife, Carolyn, and I would use to rear our two children for awhile, one of the few available rentals in the north end of the city, a preferred address for those who enjoy large old mansion-style homes, built by those who made it in the rush for Cripple Creek gold near the turn of the century.

I got out of the car and looked at the house. It was hard to believe — $115 a month, about 25% of my starting salary. I would be a "Clark," the senior partner's English pronunciation of clerk, for the next four months until I received my Colorado license, (assuming, of course, that I'd passed the test).

The home was two-storied, three bedrooms, a large porch, located in the established and posh part of north end Colorado Springs — and it was red with a fireplace.

In the years that followed, I met with clients daily, wrote their wills and trusts when appropriate, tried a passel of cases for them, held their hands at their bedsides in nursing centers and hospitals when they were ill or dying, hopelessly incompetent and demented, and listened to all of them. In every event, at least as I have grown older, my purpose has been to make the lives of those who filled our office waiting room, less anxious, better, if I could.

#

The red house is still there, the same color. It's fun to drive by it, which I'm able to do whenever I'm in the Springs' north end. Our first home looks exactly the same as it did in 1963, and there is a secure feeling that I get from that. And I can still hear my four-year-old son asking his Daddy, to "get a red house, with a fireplace," as he waved goodbye to me as I boarded the Atchison, Topeka and Santa Fe train, pulling out of the Topeka station on that city's north side. A new life in a new place, a new beginning for our family was starting. School was out — school was just beginning.

The preceding chapters, the stories they contain — they are what I've learned in school.

"If You Want Out — See Cruz"

It is a reasonable assumption, I suggest, that very few elder law attorneys have ever found themselves in the bowels of their city's jail — as unlikely, I suppose, as an elder lawyer occupying her or his time in contemplating boolean notations. "Boolean," as we all know, is a system of algebraic notation used to represent logical propositions by means of the binary digits (0) and (1).

In the days prior to the creation of public defender offices in our states and communities, our local bar association mandated that pro-bono services be performed by all lawyers. Judges would assign this duty to us, ignoring our inability to confidently protect our assigned clients' personal interests. Essentially, this interest was to keep them out of the hoosegow using a deserving defense.

Not yet dry behind the ears, I was just out of law school when the mandate to defend those accused of crime, impecunious and entitled to a free defense, was ordered.

#

The telephone rang. I answered it. The chief judge in our county was on the line. I'd been in his court a few times. He was a good judge and not one you could refuse.

"I'm assigning a case to you," he said. "He's in the jail."

"Tom" — I've forgotten the last name — was the accused's lawyer, but the guy in the black and white horizontally-striped jail garb didn't like him. He wanted another lawyer, somebody good. Tom was the best criminal defense lawyer in town in those days, the early 60's. He'd been a D.A. and was now into big fee defense. Because this was a no-fee appointment, Tom had undoubtedly lost interest in the case and figured out a plan to avoid having to defend. Tom was the best in town. I knew what this judge was doing. "You don't like the best we've got — see how you like the worst." I qualified for that title.

Criminal law — that was my only "C" grade in law school, a required class and one in which I had little interest. This real life criminal was getting reamed; the judge was seeing to that. His defender was below average, way below.

"Get down to the jail," the judge ordered. "Tell this guy to keep his hands clean" — whatever that meant. So I did; I headed for the pokey.

In what was the basement of the jailhouse, a small room had been constructed — four or five feet wide and about twice that in length. A buzzer was just inside the entrance. One was to push that button when the conference was over. At the far end was a small desk and chair. That's where the lawyer sat — eight feet away from the buzzer, and the accused sat or stood in front of the lawyer and the desk, near the buzzer.

If the presumed bad guy wasn't ready to leave, there was no way that the lawyer could get the buzzer pushed. It was scary.

I stood outside the small room's entrance with a guard until my first criminal client arrived. He was huge, the largest man I'd ever seen. He could have filled two spaces on any pro football team's offensive line. He was so tall that I had to crook my neck upward to see his face. We went into the room. The door was locked from the outside, and the guard meandered away.

This was my first criminal case.

"Okay," I said, looking up at this brute. "What did ya do?"

"Nothing," he responded.

"Okay," I said, "I believe you. Ring the buzzer." He did. The guard came. The door was opened; I left.

Back at the office the phone rang. It was the judge.

"Kruse," he said, "I've got to dismiss the case." He explained some technical reason for this erasing of the charge — whatever it might have been. I have no idea what my response was, but I was thrilled. There is a God, I reasoned.

"Go back to the jail and tell your client to keep his hands clean."

"Why, Judge? Just let him out," I said, to which there was no discernable response, so I headed for the jail once again to see this unfrozen mammoth. Back to the basement, led to the buzzer room, I stood outside awaiting the behemoth's arrival.

"Okay," I said when he arrived, "you're free," and I turned and left.

#

The second phone call of the morning was from the sheriff.

"Cruz," he said, "what the hell did you do?"

"What do you mean?" I wondered aloud. Perhaps the buzzer was broken, poked and ruined by the smallest finger of the giant who had been my client.

"It's written all over my jail's walls — everywhere," he said. "If you want out — see Cruz."

#

Fortunately for the criminal population in Colorado Springs, the public defender system was enacted in our state. Real defense lawyers were hired to represent those among us who were found to be in need of protection. And so I had my first criminal case behind me. I was assigned others, of course, as was every other lawyer in our community — but having my wits literally scared out of me in my first case — those that followed were, in comparison, pretty mellow.

In the only other notable defense in which I had an assigned part, a young man was accused of theft. A small grocery store was robbed, and this wanderer and his colleagues locked up the employees in the freezer — 10 or 12 of them. Of course, they all testified that my client, indeed, was the robber, the one who had done the dastardly deed. And he was quickly disposed of. I didn't have much of a defense. He stunk to high heaven, and I shared my fee with another young lawyer after the first day of trial just to sit between him and me at the counsel's table so I could breathe. The smell was pungent. Of course, we lost, and this vagabond was transported back to his cage. Shortly thereafter, he was diagnosed as having syphilis of the brain. He sent me a letter from prison, having been moved from the jailhouse to the big house. I dreaded opening it assuming that I was being blamed — appropriately, of course, for the loss.

"Dear Cruz, I just [want to] thank you," he wrote, "and the other guy for helping me." That was it, the full letter. I memorized the contents, "thank you for helping me," not knowing whether to attribute his thoughtful missive to the disease or not; after all, syphilis adversely affects the carrier's brain.

Shortly after this episode, however, I was freed — no longer a servant dispensing advice to behemoths charged with crimes. The public defender system arrived in Colorado, and, fortunately for us all, well-trained defense attorneys took over — and presumably the jail walls got washed as well.